A GUIDE TO PROGRAMMING IN APPLE SOFT

LAWRENCEVILLE PRESS, INC.

BRUCE PRESLEY

DISTRIBUTED BY

VNR VAN NOSTRAND REINHOLD COMPANY
NEW YORK CINCINNATI TORONTO LONDON MELBOURNE

First published in 1982

Library of Congress Catalog Card Numer 81-52974

ISBN 0-442-25890-9

VNR

Van Nostrand Reinhold Company
135 West 50th Street, New York, NY 10020

Van Nostrand Reinhold Ltd.
1410 Birchmount Road, Scarborough, Ontario M1P 2E7

Van Nostrand Reinhold Australia Pty. Ltd.
17 Queen Street, Mitcham, Victoria 3132

Van Nostrand Reinhold Company Ltd.
Molly Millars Lane, Wokingham, Berkshire, England RG11 2PY

16 15 14 13 12 11 10 9 8 7 6 5 4

PREFACE

The publication of this first edition of A GUIDE TO PROGRAMMING IN APPLESOFT represents the latest achievement of faculty members and students at The Lawrenceville School in developing curricular materials to assist students in learning to program computers.

Based on experience gained in our classrooms over the past ten years, we are convinced that a structured, concisely written computer text is invaluable in teaching and learning programming. This latest manual, written specifically to instruct students in Applesoft, not only retains but expands on the features which have resulted in the wide acceptance of our previous publication, A GUIDE TO PROGRAMMING IN BASIC PLUS.

The production of this manual has involved the cooperation and talents of many individuals. Lawrenceville faculty members Stuart Hayes and William Graupner, along with former Lawrenceville students John Partridge, Lester Waters, David Hayden and Robert Lynch, have all made contributions to this publication which have been invaluable. Each has authored and taken responsibility for specific areas of the manual. The clarity and accuracy of each chapter reflect their considerable effort and expertise. Marjorie Vining, of the Rhode Island School of Design, has produced the imaginative cover design and art work, while Dr. Theodore Fraser of The College of the Holy Cross has edited the text to ensure that it is both grammatically and stylistically correct.

To all of these people I am deeply grateful. Thanks to their combined efforts, we have produced what I believe to be one of the very finest computer texts available today.

Bruce W. Presley

TABLE OF CONTENTS

1

INTRODUCTION TO PROGRAMMING

To communicate with a computer a special language is required. The language of the APPLE computer is called APPLESOFT BASIC which consists of simple English words that the computer understands. In this chapter the user will be introduced to the most fundamental statements required to write a program on the APPLE.

What Is a Program?

A program is a sequence of instructions that informs the computer of the tasks which the user wants it to perform. From the very beginning it is important to realize that the user must determine the order in which the computer performs all tasks assigned to it. It is also essential to realize that the computer operates with a limited vocabulary and that it can understand only certain key words which serve as commands. Hence, words which make perfect sense to the user may make no sense at all to the computer if they are not part of its vocabulary. It is the purpose of this manual to teach one of the special vocabularies of the APPLE and to explain how it can be used in a variety of ways.

Line Numbering

To establish the sequence of instructions for any given program, line numbers must first be assigned to each line of the program. This operation is essential since the computer reads instructions beginning with the lowest line number, then progresses to the next higher number, and ends with the highest numbered line.

It is permissible to type the program lines out of order because the computer puts them back into their proper order. For example, line 20 may have been typed before line 10; but, when the program is run, the computer automatically reads line 10 first. Such a system has the advantage of allowing any forgotten instructions, say between lines 10 and 20, to be entered later as lines 15, or 12, or 17, etc. For this reason it is best to number the lines of the program in units of ten (10, 20, 30, etc.) since this leaves nine possible line numbers that can later be inserted. It is also important to realize that the capital letter O cannot be used in place of zero.

An error in any instruction may be corrected at any time by depressing the return key and retyping the entire line, using the same line number. If two lines are given the same line number, the computer uses only the last one typed and ignores the first. Typing only a line number followed by a RETURN eliminates that line entirely. The highest line number allowed on the APPLE is 63999.

PRINT

There are two basic types of information which the APPLE can utilize: numbers and words. What distinguishes one from the other is that a number can be used in a mathematical calculation, whereas a word cannot. The PRINT statement is used to print both numbers and words.

PROGRAM 1.1

This program uses the PRINT statement at each line to print the results shown below.

```
10   PRINT 5 * 3
20   PRINT 12 + 8
30   PRINT 7 / 2
40   PRINT "JONES"
50   PRINT "5*3"

]RUN
15
20
3.5
JONES
5*3
```

Line 10 instructs the computer to print the result of 5 multiplied by 3. Note that an asterisk (*) is used to indicate multiplication. Line 20 adds 12 and 8 while line 30 divides 7 by 2, with the slash (/) indicating division. At line 40 the word JONES is printed. To be printed, a word or any set of characters must be enclosed within quotation marks. Line 50 prints 5*3 rather than 15 because quotation marks are used. Information which is enclosed in quotation marks is called a string. Both lines 40 and 50, for example, contain strings.

The command RUN is typed after a program has been completed to cause the programmed instructions to be executed. It is not part of the program.

Typing Errors

An error in a program can be corrected in one of two ways. First, the program line can be retyped using the same line number. For example,

```
]40 PRINT "SMITH"

]RUN
15
20
3.5
SMITH
5*3
```

changes only that part of the output of Program 1.1 which is produced by line 40. The second method of correcting an error uses the keys marked → and ← and may be used if the error is detected while the line containing the error is being typed. Pressing the ← key a sufficient number of times will move the cursor on the screen back to the location of the error, where typing the correct symbol will replace the error. Pressing the → key will bring the cursor to the end of the incomplete line so that typing can resume.

LIST

The LIST command is used to print the program currently in the computer's memory. Typing LIST followed by a RETURN will print the entire program, while LIST followed by a line number and a RETURN will cause only that line to be printed. To list portions of a program type LIST followed by the first and last line numbers of the portion desired, separating the two numbers with a hyphen (-). For example:

```
]LIST

10  PRINT 5 * 3
20  PRINT 12 + 8
30  PRINT 7 / 2
40  PRINT "JONES"
50  PRINT "5*3"

]LIST 50

50  PRINT "5*3"

]LIST 20-40

20  PRINT 12 + 8
30  PRINT 7 / 2
40  PRINT "JONES"
```

NEW

Before entering a program into the computer, the NEW command should be used to clear the computer's memory. The use of this command insures that program lines from a previous program do not affect the new program.

```
]LIST

10   PRINT 5 * 3
20   PRINT 12 + 8
30   PRINT 7 / 2
40   PRINT "JONES"
50   PRINT "5*3"

]NEW

]LIST


]
```

Observe that after the NEW command is used, a subsequent LIST shows that no program is currently in the computer's memory.

What Is a Variable?

One of the most useful properties of a computer is its ability to manipulate variables. A variable is a symbol that may assume many different values. The computer uses variables to represent numbers or strings.

Numeric variables are represented by letters or by letters and numbers. A, D, A1, and B1 are all legal names for numeric variables. The APPLE allows the use of long names for variables, but for the sake of simplicity only a single letter or a single letter followed by a single digit will be used in the early chapters of this manual.

Variables can change in value as the name itself implies. For example, suppose that program line

20 X = 5

is typed. When the program is run and reaches line 20, X will be assigned the value 5. Suppose a later statement such as

50 X = 7

is typed. Then at line 50 the value of X will change from 5 to 7.

Just as in algebra, the computer can have one numeric variable defined in terms of another. For example, if Y = 4*X, then Y will equal 20 when X = 5, and Y will equal 28 when X = 7.

PROGRAM 1.2

This program assigns values to the variables X and Y, where Y depends upon X.

```
10 X = 12
20 Y = 3 * X + 5
30  PRINT X,Y
40 X = 15
50 Y = 3 * X + 5
60  PRINT X,Y

]RUN
12              41
15              50
```

The value of X is originally 12 at line 10 and then becomes 15 at line 40. Y changes its value at line 50 because X changed at line 40. Note also that a comma used in the PRINT statements at lines 30 and 60 allow both the values of X and Y to be printed on a single line. Note also that up to three variables can be printed on a single line by the use of commas to separate their respective names.

String variable names are used in the same way as numeric variable names, except that a string variable name must end with a dollar sign ($). For example, A$, D$,A1$,C5$ all represent string variables. To assign characters to a string variable the characters must be enclosed in quotation marks. For example,

10 A$ = "HARRY"

At some point later in a program it is possible to assign different characters to the variable. For example,

50 A$ = "SALLY"

PROGRAM 1.3

This program assigns two different sets of characters to the string variable B$.

```
10 B$ = "GEORGE"
20  PRINT B$
30 B$ = "JUDY"
40  PRINT B$
50  PRINT "IT IS NICE TO SEE YOU ";B$

]RUN
GEORGE
JUDY
IT IS NICE TO SEE YOU JUDY
```

Observe that at line 50 a sentence can be formed from two strings, the first of which is not given a variable name. Also, observe how the blank spaces in the first string affect what is printed.

REVIEW

1. Write a program that will print the value of Y when Y = 5X + 7 and X = 5.
2. Write a program that will produce the following output, using a single string variable names for "HARRY" and "JUDY" but not for the other words.

```
]RUN
HELLO HARRY
HOW ARE YOU?
JUDY IS LOOKING FOR YOU.
```

READ, DATA

A variable may be directly assigned its value not only by means of a statement such as X = 5, but also by the use of a combination of READ and DATA statements.

PROGRAM 1.4

This program uses READ and DATA statements to assign values to numeric variables.

```
10   READ X,Y,Z
20   PRINT 2 * X + 3 * Y + 8 * Z
30   DATA  3,2,0.5

]RUN
16
```

The READ statement at line 10 instructs the computer to assign numbers to the variables X, Y, Z. The computer finds these numbers in the DATA statement at line 30 and assigns them in the order listed (X = 3, Y = 2, and Z = 0.5).

In a DATA statement only numbers that are expressed in decimal or scientific form are acceptable. For example, the numbers .0032, -5.78, 1050, 2.9E5, and 4.76 E-12 are acceptable. The E stands for "times ten to the power" (e.g., 5.3 E3 = 5300 and 8.72 E-3 = .00872). However, data such as the arithmetic expressions 15/3, 3*5, and 7+2 are not permitted in DATA statements since, unlike PRINT statements, DATA statements allow for no calculations.

GOTO

Suppose that a student has more than one set of values to substitute for the variables X, Y, Z in Program 1.4. To introduce the extra values, line 30 can be retyped as follows:

```
]30 DATA 3,2,0.5,-7,2.5,1E2

]RUN
16
```

Note that while only the first three numbers in the DATA statement are processed, the remaining numbers are not used. To overcome this problem, line 30 could be retyped each time a new set of data is to be run, but this involves unnecessary labor. By including a GOTO statement between lines 20 and 30, the problem can be more easily solved by establishing a loop which allows line 10 to be used over again.

```
]LIST

10  READ X,Y,Z
20  PRINT 2 * X + 3 * Y + 8 * Z
25  GOTO 10
30  DATA  3,2,0.5,-7,2.5,1E2

]RUN
16
793.5

?OUT OF DATA ERROR IN 10
```

Observe that by typing the command LIST, the computer prints the current version of Program 1.4 including the new line. Running Program 1.4 now processes all of the data presented in line 30. Each time the computer reaches line 25, the GOTO statement causes the computer to return to line 10 where the next set of data is assigned to the variables. On the first pass through the loop X = 3, Y = 2, Z = .5; on the second pass X = −7, Y = 2.5, Z = 1E2. However, on the third attempted pass, no additional data is present for assignment to the variables at line 10, and therefore the error message is printed.

The location of the DATA statement within a program is not important; it can be placed anywhere. When the computer encounters a READ statement it makes use of the DATA statement regardless of its location. The DATA statement may contain strings as well as numbers.

PROGRAM 1.5

This program reads the names and grades of three students and prints the averages of their grades.

```
5  PRINT "NAME","AVERAGE"
10  READ N$,A,B,C,D
20 X = (A + B + C + D) / 4
30  PRINT N$,X
40  GOTO 10
50  DATA  WATERS,83,75,52,80,PARTRIDGE,74,81,92,76,HAYDEN,72,81,63,60

]RUN
NAME               AVERAGE
WATERS             72.5
PARTRIDGE          80.75
HAYDEN             69

?OUT OF DATA ERROR IN 10
```

Examine this program carefully since it contains a number of important concepts. First, note that line 5 produces the headings for the columns. It is placed at the beginning of the program to insure that the headings will only be printed once. Second, note that line 10 assigns a student's name to the string variable N$ and the student's four grades to the numeric variables A, B, C, D. Unless the sequence of string variables and numeric variables in the READ statement is the same as the sequence of strings and numbers in the DATA statement, an error will occur. Third, line 40 returns the program to line 10 to continue to read data. What would happen if at line 40 the statement read GOTO 5 instead of 10?

REVIEW

3. Write a program using READ, DATA statements to evaluate Y where Y = 3X + 5 and X = 3, 5, 12, 17, 8.

4. Write a program containing the DATA line in Program 1.5 which prints only the name and first grade of each student.

```
]RUN
NAME                FIRST GRADE
WATERS              83
PARTRIDGE           74
HAYDEN              72
```

INPUT

In many instances it is preferable to introduce data from the keyboard rather than placing it in a DATA statement. To do this an INPUT statement is used in place of the READ, DATA statements. When an INPUT statement is executed the computer prints a question mark (?) and then waits for data to be entered.

PROGRAM 1.6

Data input from the keyboard is used to assign a value to the variable X in the following program.

```
10   INPUT X
20   PRINT 5 * X * X + 3 * X + 2
30   GOTO 10

]RUN
?3
56
?6
200
?2
28
?

BREAK IN 10
```

The GOTO statement at line 30 creates a loop which will continue to run until it is interrupted by a CONTROL C. To execute CONTROL C, press the CTRL and C keys simultaneously, then press the RETURN key. This halts the run of the program and causes BREAK IN 10 to be printed. If this were not done, Program 1.6 would continue to run until the reset key was pressed or the computer shut off.

PROGRAM 1.7

This program is a revision of Program 1.5. Here a student is asked for his or her name and four grades. The computer then prints the name and grade average. Note that it is possible to have the INPUT statement print a question or a remark by enclosing the words to be printed in quotation marks followed by a semicolon and the variable names.

```
10   INPUT "WHAT IS YOUR NAME? ";N$
20   INPUT "WHAT ARE YOUR FOUR GRADES? ";A,B,C,D
30 X = (A + B + C + D) / 4
40   PRINT N$,X
50   GOTO 10

]RUN
WHAT IS YOUR NAME? SANDRA
WHAT ARE YOUR FOUR GRADES? 78,82,69,75
SANDRA          76
WHAT IS YOUR NAME? JAKE
WHAT ARE YOUR FOUR GRADES? 80,65,79,77
JAKE            75.25
WHAT IS YOUR NAME? TOM
WHAT ARE YOUR FOUR GRADES? 67,53,72,68
TOM             65
WHAT IS YOUR NAME?

BREAK IN 10
```

PRINT Formatting

There are a number of ways in which output can be formatted by the use of punctuation. A few of the more important uses of punctuation are demonstrated by the following program.

PROGRAM 1.8

When using most video displays the APPLE is capable of printing 40 characters on a single line. The number will differ with many paper printers. When the print line consists of 40 characters, this line is divided into three print zones: the first and second are 16 characters wide, the third 8 characters wide. When commas are used in a PRINT statement the output is printed in successive zones.

```
5   PRINT "NAME","GRADES","AVERAGE"
10   READ N$,A,B,C,D
20 X = (A + B + C + D) / 4
30   PRINT
40   PRINT N$,A;" ";B;" ";C;" ";D;"      ";X
50   GOTO 10
60   DATA  WATERS,83,75,52,80,PARTRIDGE,74,81,92,76,HAYDEN,72,81,63,60
```

```
]RUN
NAME                GRADES              AVERAGE

WATERS              83 75 52 80         72.5

PARTRIDGE           74 81 92 76         80.75

HAYDEN              72 81 63 60         69

?OUT OF DATA ERROR IN 10
```

Note the output produced by line 5. Each word begins at the beginning of one of the three zones because commas have been used to separate the words. The PRINT at line 30 is used to place a blank line between each of the printed lines. When semicolons (;) are used in place of commas as on line 40, the output for each variable begins in the next space after the printing of the previous variable. This is why the quotation marks are required in line 40 to give a single space between each grade. If line 40 were changed to

```
40 PRINT N$; A; B; C; D; X
```

the output would appear as follows.

```
]RUN
NAME                GRADES              AVERAGE

WATERS8375528072.5

PARTRIDGE7481927680.75

HAYDEN7281636069

?OUT OF DATA ERROR IN 10
```

REVIEW

5. Write a program in which you input a value of X and have the computer calculate 5*X and X/5. The printout should appear exactly as shown below.

```
]RUN
?12
5*X= 60
X/5= 2.4
?2
5*X= 10
X/5= .4
?5
5*X= 25
X/5= 1
?

BREAK IN 10
```

6. Write a program which allows you to input your name and the name of a friend and then produces the printout as follows.

```
]RUN
WHAT IS YOUR NAME? BRUCE
WHAT IS YOUR FRIEND'S NAME? JUDY
JUDY IS A FRIEND OF BRUCE

WHAT IS YOUR NAME? SALLY
WHAT IS YOUR FRIEND'S NAME? MARY
MARY IS A FRIEND OF SALLY

WHAT IS YOUR NAME?

BREAK IN 10
```

Immediate Mode

The APPLE may perform simple tasks using the immediate mode rather than a program. An immediate mode instruction is typed without a line number. When the computer receives a command without a line number, it recognizes that the command is not part of a program to be run later, but one to be executed immediately. The following are examples of immediate mode statements.

```
]PRINT (3*5)+4
19

]PRINT 7/9
.777777778

]A=5

]B=2

]PRINT A+B+4
11

]A$="HOWARD"

]PRINT A$;" JONES"
HOWARD JONES
```

Note that a RUN command is not used in any of the preceding examples. Most Applesoft commands are permissible in the immediate mode with notable exceptions being the INPUT and READ, DATA statements. It is best to write complete programs to perform most tasks on the APPLE and reserve the use of immediate mode for simple calculations.

REM

The REM statement is used in the body of a program to allow the programmer to introduce explanatory remarks. Everything to the right of a REM statement is ignored by the computer when the program is run. REM statements are not printed by the computer. For example,

```
30 REM THIS PROGRAM WAS WRITTEN BY JOHNNY APPLESEED
```

will appear only in the body of the program.

EXERCISES

PART A

1. Write a program which prints the following.

```
]RUN
A
 B
  C
ABCD
```

2. Write a program which makes the following calculations. Check the results by hand computation.

   (a) 8 * (19 - 4)
   (b) 1 * 2 + 2 * 3 + 3 * 4 + 4 * 5
   (c) 1 + 1 / 10 + 1 / 100
   (d) 10 - 20 + 30 - 40 + 50 - 60

3. What is the exact output for the following program?

```
10 A = 3
20  PRINT "THE VALUE OF B"
30 B = A + 4 * 4
40  PRINT B
```

4. How many lines of output does the following program produce before an error message appears indicating "?OUT OF DATA ERROR IN 10"?

```
10   READ A,B,C
20   PRINT (A + B + C) / 3
30   GOTO 10
40   DATA   11,32,43,14,25,36,47
50   DATA   58,39,50,61,22,83,94
```

5. Peter Kolodnigork has loused up once again. Here is a program of his which he says "mysteriously doesn't work". Give Peter a hand and correct this monstrosity for him so that the output looks like the following:

```
THE SUM IS 20
THE SUM IS 14
?OUT OF DATA ERROR IN 10
```

```
10   READ A B
20   PRINT THE SUM IS  A+B
30   GOTO 12
40   DATA 12,8,3*3,5
```

6. Write the output, and check by running the program.

```
10  DATA  S,I,X!," 6",6
20  READ A$
30  PRINT A$
40  GOTO 20
```

7. Write a program in which the price (P) in cents of a loaf of bread and the number (N) of loaves bought are entered from the keyboard. The total spent for bread is to be printed in dollars and cents.

8. Write a program to enter your weight (W) in pounds and height (H) in inches and which then prints the quotient W/H followed by the words "POUNDS PER INCH".

9. Using an INPUT statement, write a program which produces the following output.

```
]RUN
?2,4
X=2                    Y=4                    X*Y=8
?-8,70
X=-8                   Y=70                   X*Y=-560
?
```

10. Predict the output of the following program. Check the answer by running the program.

```
10 P$ = "TOTAL PRICE"
20 P = .89
30  PRINT P$;" = $0";P
```

11. Write the output, and check by running the program.

```
10  READ A,B,C,D
20  PRINT A,B
30  PRINT C;"   ";D
40  DATA  3E2,510,3E-1,.51
```

12. Use immediate mode to print the following numbers.

(a) .05 (b) .005
(c) 123456789 (d) 1234567890
(e) –.065 (f) 4.62E5
(g) .086E-3 (h) –4,900

13. Self-proclaimed computer whiz Cecil Cedric Cenceless has typed up the following gibberish in the immediate mode and has challenged anyone to guess the output correctly before he or she presses the RETURN key. Put Cecil in his place and correctly predict the answer.

```
PRINT "AAA";111,222;"AAA","333";"    ";16-3*2
```

14. Write a program which will add the numbers 3, 5, and 7.

PART B

15. What is the exact output for the following program?

```
10 A$ = "ABCD"
20 B$ = "XYZ"
30 F = 7
40 G =  - 4
50  PRINT A$;B$
60  PRINT A$;F
70  PRINT F;B$
80  PRINT G;B$
```

16. Write a program to evaluate each of the following expressions for A = 10 and B = 7.

$$(7A + 10B)/2AB \qquad\qquad (1/2)A/(A-B)$$

17. In the first week of the season the cross country team ran the following number of miles each day: 2, 3, 4, 3, 5. Write a program to calculate and print the total mileage for the week.

18. A piece of pizza normally contains about 375 calories. A person jogging one mile uses about 100 calories. Write a program that asks a person how many pieces he or she wishes to eat and then tells him/her how far they must run to burn up the calories they will consume.

```
]RUN
HOW MANY PIECES DID YOU EAT? 4
YOU MUST RUN 15 MILES.
```

19. Have the computer evaluate the expression 12x + 7y for the following data:

x	3	7	12
y	2	9	–4

20. The art of thinking up good insults can be enormously aided by the computer. To test an insult, have a computer program ask for the victim's name and the insulting word which should then be attached to the suffixes "breath" and "head". For example, given "Gary" as the victim's name and "bone" as the insulting word, the program should print:

GARY IS A BONE-HEAD
or
GARY IS A BONE-BREATH

21. Using an INPUT statement, write a program that will compute the volume of a room given its length, width, and height.

22. Write a program to compute the areas (cm^2) of circles with radii 5.0 cm., 3.0 cm., and 8.0 cm. Have the output in the form "AREA OF CIRCLE =" with two spaces between each of the printed lines.

23. Just as three-dimensional objects are measured by volume, so four-dimensional objects are measured by tesseracts. Have your program ask for the dimensions of a four-dimensional object, height, width, length, and "presence" and print the object's tesseract.

24. With the equation of $E = MC^2$, Einstein showed that energy could be produced from matter. If the average human hair weighs a tenth of a gram and the town of Woodsylvania uses 2×10^{11} units of energy in a day, find out how many hairs from Einstein's head would be required to supply the town for a day ($C = 3 \times 10^{10}$).

25. Use the computer to calculate your library fines. Enter the number of books you have borrowed and how many days late they are. Have the computer print the amount of your fine if you are charged 10¢ per day per book.

26. The perimeter of a triangle is equal to the sum of the lengths of the three sides of the triangle. The semiperimeter is one-half of the perimeter. A triangle has sides of lengths 13 cm, 8 cm, 11 cm. A second triangle has sides of 21 ft, 16 ft, 12 ft. Write a program that reads these measurements from a DATA statement and then prints the semiperimeter of each triangle showing the correct units. The output should look like this:

```
SEMIPERIMETER OF FIRST TRIANGLE  16 CM.

SEMIPERIMETER OF SECOND TRIANGLE  24.5 FT.
```

27. Professional athletes have succeeded in making staggering sums of money through careful negotiations. Of course, the real winner is Uncle Sam who does not negotiate at all. Write a program which asks for a player's name and salary and then prints the player's name, take-home salary, and taxes if the tax rate for his income bracket is 44%.

28. Sale prices are often deceptive. Write a program to determine the original price of an item, given the sale price and the discount rate.

29. The area of a triangle can be found by multiplying one-half times the length of the base times the length of the altitude (A = .5 x base x height). Write a program that allows the user to enter from the keyboard the base and altitude of a triangle and then skips a line before printing out the area of the triangle.

```
]RUN
WHAT IS THE BASE? 8
WHAT IS THE ALTITUDE? 5

THE AREA IS 20
```

30. A state has a 7 percent sales tax. Write a program that will allow you to INPUT the names and prices (before taxes) of different items found in a department store and then print the item, tax, and the price of the item including tax.

31. In an election in Grime City, candidate Sloth ran against candidate Graft for mayor. Below is a listing of the number of votes both candidates received in each ward. What total vote did each candidate receive? What percentage of the total vote did each candidate receive?

Candidate	Sloth	Graft
Ward 1	528	210
2	313	721
3	1003	822
4	413	1107
5	516	1700

32. A Susan B. Anthony dollar of diameter 2.6 centimeters rests on a square postage stamp as shown. Have the computer find the area in square centimeters of the part of the stamp not covered by the coin.

33. Given the assumption that you sleep a healthy 8 hours a night, have the computer print the number of hours of your life which you have spent sleeping. Input the date of your birth and today's date in numeric form (e.g., 6, 4, 62). Use 365 days in each year and 30 days in a month.

34. Using an INPUT statement, write a program which averages each of the following sets of numbers (2, 7, 15, 13); (8, 5, 2, 3); (12, 19, 4); (15, 7, 19, 24, 37). Note that the sets do not contain the same number of elements.

2 DECISIONS AND LOOPS

The statements presented in Chapter One allow the APPLE to perform routine calculations and to print numbers or strings in different formats. The higher capabilities of a computer are not called upon however, until the computer is used to make decisions or to carry out a process many times. This chapter presents the conditional statement (IF . . . THEN) which allows the computer to make decisions and the statements (FOR . . . TO . . . STEP, NEXT) which establish a loop in the most convenient manner.

IF . . . THEN

The statements introduced in Chapter One (GOTO, PRINT, etc.) are called unconditional because the computer must process them in the order of their occurrence. In contrast, the IF . . . THEN statement is conditional because the action it takes depends upon whether or not some test statement is found to be true.

The general form for the IF . . . THEN statement is

IF <condition> THEN <line number>

The "condition" portion of the statement compares two quantities which must be separated by one of the symbols indicated in the table below.

SYMBOL	MEANING
=	equal to
>	greater than
<	less than
>=	greater than or equal to
<=	less than or equal to
<>	not equal to

An example of an IF . . . THEN statement is:

```
20 IF X>5 THEN 60
```

When the condition in line 20 (X is greater than 5) is true, the computer jumps to line 60. When the condition is false because X is less than or equal to 5, the computer proceeds to the next line of the program.

PROGRAM 2.1

This program determines whether an input value of X is the solution to the equation 2X - 18 = 0. The computer decides which of two messages is to be printed.

```
10   INPUT X
20   IF 2 * X - 18 = 0 THEN 50
30   PRINT X;" IS NOT THE SOLUTION"
40   GOTO 10
50   PRINT X;" IS THE SOLUTION"

]RUN
?15
15 IS NOT THE SOLUTION
?4
4 IS NOT THE SOLUTION
?9
9 IS THE SOLUTION

]
```

Note the necessity of line 40. Without it, the program would print "IS THE SOLUTION" even when the solution was not X. The line number sequence that the computer follows when X is the solution is 10, 20, 50, and when X is *not* the solution it follows the line number sequence 10, 20, 30, 40, 10.

The IF . . . THEN statement can be used to compare strings of letters. Here symbols greater than (>), less than (<), equal (=), etc., now refer to an alphabetical rather than a numerical order.

PROGRAM 2.2

The following program determines whether A$ is alphabetically before, after, or the same as B$.

```
10   PRINT
20   INPUT "ENTER TWO STRINGS? ";A$,B$
30   IF A$ = B$ THEN 70
40   IF A$ > B$ THEN 90
50   PRINT A$;" IS BEFORE ";B$
60   GOTO 10
70   PRINT A$;" IS EQUIVALENT TO ";B$
80   GOTO 10
90   PRINT A$;" IS AFTER ";B$
100   GOTO 10

]RUN

ENTER TWO STRINGS? A,C
A IS BEFORE C

ENTER TWO STRINGS? DEC,CDC
DEC IS AFTER CDC

ENTER TWO STRINGS? CHRIS,CHRIS
CHRIS IS EQUIVALENT TO CHRIS

ENTER TWO STRINGS?

BREAK IN 20
```

Line 30 directs the computer to line 70 if A$ and B$ are equivalent. Line 40 causes a jump to line 90 if A$ comes after B$ in the alphabet. Line 50 is reached only if both conditions in lines 30 and 40 fail and, therefore, A$ comes before B$ in the alphabet.

Extended Use of the IF . . . Statement, Multiple Statement Lines

In the preceding section the general form of the IF . . . THEN statement was given as:

IF <condition> THEN <line number>

More flexible usage of IF . . . THEN permits a statement instead of a line number to follow the word THEN. The statement after the condition will be executed only if the condition is true. The form is:

IF <condition> THEN <statement>

The following examples illustrate legal uses of the IF . . . THEN statement:

IF X<>0 THEN PRINT X

IF Z>1 THEN PRINT "IT IS LARGER THAN ONE"

IF R<=0 THEN R = X + 2

Applesoft Basic allows a series of statements to be entered on a single line if they are separated from each other by colons (:). Multiple statement lines have special meaning when used with IF . . . THEN. *All* statements following THEN will be executed when the condition following IF is true. *No* statements following THEN will be executed when the condition is false. For example,

60 IF X = 5 THEN PRINT "GOOD" : GOTO 80

has two statements on one line. If the condition X = 5 is true, then "GOOD" will be printed and program control will be passed to line 80. If the condition is not true, neither of these actions is taken. Instead, the program will continue on to the line following line 60. This means either both the PRINT "GOOD" and the GOTO 80 statements are executed, or else neither is executed. Whichever of the two occurs depends upon whether the condition X = 5 be true or false.

PROGRAM 2.3

Program 2.1 can be shortened by using multiple statement techniques.

```
10   INPUT X
20   IF 2 * X - 18 = 0 THEN  PRINT X;" IS THE SOLUTION": GOTO 10
30   PRINT X;" IS NOT THE SOLUTION": GOTO 10

]RUN
?15
15 IS NOT THE SOLUTION
?2
2 IS NOT THE SOLUTION
?9
9 IS THE SOLUTION
?

BREAK IN 10
```

Note that the statement GOTO 10 in line 20 is executed *only* if the condition in the IF . . . THEN statement is true. Otherwise the program proceeds to line 30. The statement GOTO 10 on line 30 will always be executed if line 30 is reached since it is not preceded by an IF . . . THEN statement on the same line.

AND, OR

The statement modifiers AND and OR can be used in the IF . . . THEN statement when more than one condition is to be considered. The statement

```
20 IF X>5 AND Y=3 THEN 50
```

will cause a transfer to line 50 only if both conditions are true. On the other hand, the statement

```
20 IF X>5 OR Y=3 THEN 50
```

will cause program control to be transferred to line 50 if either or both conditions are true.

PROGRAM 2.4

The following program uses the OR modifier and reviews much of what has been presented.

```
10   INPUT "WHO ARE YOU? ";N$
20   IF N$ = "JAMES BOND" OR N$ = "007" THEN 50
30   PRINT "THIS MISSION IS NOT MEANT FOR YOU!"
40   PRINT : GOTO 10
50   PRINT "THESE ORDERS ARE FOR YOUR EYES ONLY!"
60   INPUT "ARE YOU ALONE? ";A$
70   IF A$ <  > "YES" THEN  PRINT "TRY LATER.": GOTO 10
80   PRINT : PRINT "  DR. GOODHEAD HAS ESCAPED! YOUR"
90   PRINT "MISSION, SHOULD YOU DECIDE TO ACCEPT"
100   PRINT "IT, IS TO SEEK OUT GOODHEAD AND"
110   PRINT "RETURN HER TO THE TELENGARD PRISON"

]RUN
WHO ARE YOU? BRAVE SIR ROBIN
THIS MISSION IS NOT MEANT FOR YOU!

WHO ARE YOU? JAMES BOND
THESE ORDERS ARE FOR YOUR EYES ONLY!
ARE YOU ALONE? NO
TRY LATER.
WHO ARE YOU? 007
THESE ORDERS ARE FOR YOUR EYES ONLY!
ARE YOU ALONE? YES

  DR. GOODHEAD HAS ESCAPED! YOUR
MISSION, SHOULD YOU DECIDE TO ACCEPT
IT, IS TO SEEK OUT GOODHEAD AND
RETURN HER TO THE TELENGARD PRISON
```

Line 10 asks the user for a name. The name entered as N$ is compared with the two names at line 20. If N$ is either 'JAMES BOND' or '007', then the program skips to line 50. Otherwise, a message is printed by line 30, and the program returns to line 10. At line 50, a warning message is printed, while line 60 inquires whether Mr. Bond is alone or not. Note that in line 70 any response other than 'YES' will cause the program to print 'TRY LATER' and jump back to line 10. Otherwise, the mission description is printed by lines 80 through 110.

END

The END statement is used to terminate the run of a program. For example,

```
80 END
```

will cause the run of a program to stop when line 80 is reached. It is possible to place END statements at more than one location within a program, including insertion in an IF . . . THEN statement.

PROGRAM 2.5

This program uses the END statement to terminate program execution when the name KERMIT is input.

```
10   INPUT "WHAT IS YOUR NAME? ";N$
20   IF N$ = "KERMIT" THEN  END
30   PRINT "IT'S GOOD TO MEET YOU ";N$
40   PRINT : GOTO 10

]RUN
WHAT IS YOUR NAME? CYNTHIA
IT'S GOOD TO MEET YOU CYNTHIA

WHAT IS YOUR NAME? KERMIT

]
```

REVIEW

1. Allow two numbers, A and B, to be entered in the computer and then print the two numbers in descending order.

2. Allow two names to be entered and then printed in alphabetical order.

```
]RUN
ENTER TWO LAST NAMES? PATRICK, GREER
GREER
PATRICK
ENTER TWO LAST NAMES?

BREAK IN 10
```

3. Write a program that will allow a number N to be entered. If the number is between 25 and 112 then the computer should indicate this; otherwise, the computer should say that the number is out of range.

```
]RUN
ENTER A NUMBER? 14
14 IS OUT OF RANGE
ENTER A NUMBER? 54
54 IS BETWEEN 25 AND 112
ENTER A NUMBER? 112
112 IS OUT OF RANGE
ENTER A NUMBER?

BREAK IN 10
```

4. Using only one line number, enter three strings and then print them as one long string.

```
]RUN
?FIRST,SECOND,THIRD
FIRSTSECONDTHIRD
```

FOR . . . TO . . . STEP, NEXT

The FOR . . . TO . . . STEP, NEXT statements provide the simplest means for establishing a loop. They also provide a method for generating a large sequence of numbers in a case where each number in the sequence differs from its predecessor by a constant amount. The general form of the FOR . . . TO . . . STEP, NEXT statement is:

```
┌─FOR <variable> = <starting value> TO <ending value> STEP <increment>
│       •
│       •
│       •
└─NEXT <variable>
```

The STEP portion may be omitted if the increment equals +1.
For example,

```
10 FOR X = 2 TO 6
      •
      •
      •
40 NEXT X

70 FOR H1 = N*2 TO 26 STEP +2
      •
      •
      •
100 NEXT H1

120 FOR T = 10 TO 0 STEP -1
      •
      •
      •
180 NEXT T
```

Note that a loop is formed by the FOR . . . TO . . . STEP and NEXT statements.
In the example,

```
30 FOR N = 3 TO 11 STEP 2
40    •
      •
      •
80 NEXT N
```

the variable N starts at line 30 with a value of 3. N retains the value of 3 until the NEXT N statement is encountered at line 80. At this point, N is increased by the STEP value. In this example N changes from 3 to 5 to 7, etc. All the statements in the lines occurring between lines 30 and 80 are executed in sequence during each consecutive pass through the loop. The program continues to return from line 80 to line 40 until N exceeds the specified limit of 11. At this point the program exits from the loop and moves on to the line following 80.

The next two programs generate all of the integers between 10 and 30, inclusive.

PROGRAM 2.6

This program uses READ, DATA, while Program 2.7 uses a FOR . . . TO . . . STEP, NEXT loop.

```
10  READ N
20  PRINT "   ";N;
30  GOTO 10
40  PRINT "  DONE"
50  DATA  10,11,12,13,14,15,16,17,18
55  DATA  19,20,21,22,23,24,25,26,27
60  DATA  28,29,30

]RUN
  10   11   12   13   14   15   16   17   18   19   20   21   22   23   24   25   26
  27   28   29   30
?OUT OF DATA ERROR IN 10
]
```

PROGRAM 2.7

```
10  FOR N = 10 TO 30
20  PRINT "   ";N;
30  NEXT N
40  PRINT "  DONE"

]RUN
  10   11   12   13   14   15   16   17   18   19   20   21   22   23   24   25   26
  27   28   29   30   DONE

]
```

Program 2.6 continues to read data until all of it is exhausted. Program 2.7 generates all of the values of N between 10 and 30. Note that the loop in Program 2.7 is completed by a NEXT statement, not a GOTO statement. Unlike Program 2.6, Program 2.7 can therefore proceed to line 40.

PROGRAM 2.8

This program finds solutions to the compound condition 5X + 3<100 and $2X^2$>50. All odd integers from 1 to 25 are tested.

```
10  FOR X = 1 TO 25 STEP 2
20  IF 5 * X + 3 < 100 AND 2 * X ^ 2 > 50 THEN  PRINT "   ";X;
30  NEXT X
40  PRINT "  DONE"

]RUN
  7  9  11  13  15  17  19  DONE
```

Note that the symbol (^) is used to denote 'raised to the power' (e.g., X ^ 2 means X*X). Lines 10 and 30 create a loop for testing the conditions located at line 20. The loop starts at line 10 with X = 1. Each time the program reaches the NEXT X statement at line 30, N is incremented by the STEP value which is +2. The program will then return to line 20 unless the value of the loop variable X has exceeded its maximum value of 25, at which point the loop will be exited. Remember that a FOR loop is completed not by a GOTO statement, but by a NEXT statement.

REVIEW

5. Write a program that prints the integers between 1 and 25, inclusive.

6. Using a FOR .. TO ... STEP, NEXT loop, have the computer print the following:

```
]RUN
10 9 8 7 6 5 4 3 2 1
```

7. Write a program that will allow a number N to be entered. Using N as a STEP value, print numbers between 8 and 20.

```
]RUN
STEP VALUE? 2
8 10 12 14 16 18 20
```

have explained

RESTORE

At times the user might find it desirable to employ a set of data more than once. The RESTORE statement makes it possible to read data again starting at the beginning of the data. For example,

40 RESTORE

causes the next READ statement encountered to read data starting with the first item in the first DATA statement.

PROGRAM 2.9

This program searches a DATA line for a specific student and then prints the student's grades. It employs the RESTORE statement so that each time the name of a student is input the DATA line is searched from the beginning.

```
10   PRINT : INPUT "NAME? ";B$
20   RESTORE
30   FOR P = 1 TO 6
40   READ N$,A,B,C,D
50   IF N$ = B$ THEN 80
60   NEXT P
70   PRINT "STUDENT ";B$;" NOT FOUND": GOTO 10
80   PRINT N$;" HAS THE FOLLOWING GRADES:"
90   PRINT A;"   ";B;"   ";C;"   ";D
100   GOTO 10
110   DATA  WATERS,83,75,52,80,PARTRIDGE,74,81,92,76,HAYDEN,72,81,63,60
120   DATA  HAYES,99,84,92,87,GRAHAM,100,93,82,89,STEHLE,78,93,85,94

]RUN

NAME? STEHLE
STEHLE HAS THE FOLLOWING GRADES:
78  93  85  94

NAME? LYNCH
STUDENT LYNCH NOT FOUND

NAME? HAYDEN
HAYDEN HAS THE FOLLOWING GRADES:
72  81  63  60

NAME?

BREAK IN 10
```

EXERCISES

PART A

1. Write a program to allow two numbers (A and B) to be entered. Have the computer compare them and print a message stating whether A is less than, equal to, or greater than B.

2. Write a program which allows three names to be entered as A$, B$, and C$. Have the computer print the name which is alphabetically last.

3. Allow a string (A$) composed of letters to be entered. Have the computer print A$ if it comes alphabetically after the string "MIDWAY". Two line numbers and no colons are permissible.

4. Write a program which prints six exclamation marks if BIGWOW is entered for the string X$ but which otherwise prints six question marks. The program is to run until CTRL-C is used.

5. Use only one line number to enter two strings (A$ and B$) and to print output similar to the following.

```
]RUN
?START, FINISH
START           FINISH
FINISH          START
```

6. Allow a number (X) to be entered. Print the message "NOT BETWEEN" if X is either less than -24 or greater than 17. Only one IF . . . THEN statement is permitted.

7. Allow a string (A$) to be entered. Print the message "A$ IS BETWEEN" if A$ comes between "DOWN" and "UP" alphabetically. Only one IF . . . THEN statement is permitted.

8. Allow a number (X) to be entered. Print "IN THE INTERVAL" if X satisfies the inequality $25 < X < 75$, but otherwise print "NOT IN THE INTERVAL". Only one AND and one IF . . . THEN statement are to be used.

9. Rewrite the program of the preceding exercise, using OR instead of AND.

10. Use only one PRINT statement to produce the following rectangle.

```
]RUN
************
************
************
```

11. Print the cubes of the odd integers from 11 to −11, inclusive, in that order.

12. Print all the integers which end in 4 from 4 to 84, inclusive.

13. Use a loop to print a line of 40 asterisks.

14. Write a one line IMMEDIATE MODE command for each of the following:
    (A) Find the value of 143 x 74.
    (B) Find the average of 53, 72, 81, and 76.
    (C) Find which is larger, X↑Y or Y↑X, when X = 4 and Y = 5.

PART B

15. Print all of the integers in the set 10, 13, 16, 19, . . ., 94, 97.

16. Using a loop have the computer print a letter I as follows:

```
]RUN
*****
 ***
 ***
 ***
 ***
 ***
 ***
*****
```

17. Below is a list of various creatures and the weapon necessary to destroy each.

Creature	**Weapon**
Lich	Fire Ball
Mummy	Flaming Torch
Werewolf	Silver Bullet
Vampire	Wooden Stake
Medusa	Sharp Sword
Triffid	Fire Hose

Using READ and DATA, have the computer state what weapon is to be used to destroy a given creature. For example:

```
]RUN
CREATURE? MUMMY
YOU CAN KILL A MUMMY WITH A FLAMING TORCH
CREATURE? VAMPIRE
YOU CAN KILL A VAMPIRE WITH A WOODEN STAKE
CREATURE?

BREAK IN 10
]
```

18. Menacing Matilda has written the following program and cannot figure out in what order the lines of the program will be executed. Assist her by listing the line numbers in the sequence the computer will execute them.

```
10   READ A,B
20   IF A > 4 OR B > 4 THEN 50
30   IF A < 1 AND B < 1 THEN 60
40   GOTO 70
50 X = A + B: GOTO 80
60 X = A * B: GOTO 80
70 X = A / B
80   IF X > 1 THEN  PRINT X: GOTO 10
90   DATA 5,3,-1,-2,0,2
```

19. John Doe's brother Jim has been assigned the following program for homework. Jim is not in shape today, so assist him by stating the exact order in which the lines of the following program are to be executed.

```
10  READ A,B,C
20 S = A + B * C
30  IF S = 10 THEN   RESTORE : READ S
40  PRINT S,
50  IF S = 14 THEN  END
60  GOTO 10
70  DATA  4,2,3,6,0,2,7
```

20. Write a program which asks for a person's age. If the person is 16 years or older, have the computer print "YOU ARE OLD ENOUGH TO DRIVE A CAR". Otherwise, have the computer indicate how many years the person must wait before being able to drive.

```
]RUN
HOW OLD ARE YOU? 19
YOU ARE OLD ENOUGH TO DRIVE A CAR
```

21. The Happy Holiday Motel has 10 rooms. Have the computer print a label for each room's door indicating the room number. For example:

```
]RUN

-----------------------
  HAPPY HOLIDAY MOTEL
        ROOM 1
-----------------------
```

22. As candidate for mayor, you are very busy. Use the computer to print thank you letters to 10 people who have contributed money to your election campaign. Be sure to mention the exact amount each person has contributed.

```
]RUN

DEAR RICH BRYBURRY,
   THANK YOU FOR YOUR GENEROUS CONTRIBUTION
OF 25000 DOLLARS TO MY ELECTION CAMPAIGN. MAYBE
NEXT YEAR WE WILL HAVE BETTER LUCK!
                             SINCERELY,

                             SMILEY R. POLITICO
```

23. Write a program which will produce the following table:

```
]RUN
X               X^2              X^3

2               4                8
4               16               64
6               36               216
8               64               512
10              100              1000
```

24. The Bored Auto Company has done it again! Some models of their cars may be difficult to drive because their wheels are not exactly round. Cars with model numbers 102, 780, 119, 220, 189, and 195 have been found to have a defect. Write a computer program that allows 10 of their customers to enter the model number of their car to find out whether or not their car is defective.

25. Using only two print statements, write a program to print a triangle that is N lines high and N columns wide. For example:

```
]RUN
?5
*
**
***
****
*****
```

26. Have the computer find all odd integers from 5 to 25 which are simultaneous solutions of the inequalities $X^3 > 500$ and $X^2 + 3X + 2 < 700$. Print only the solutions.

27. The following table contains employee performance data for the Tippecanoe Typing Company.

Employee	**Performance**
Oakley	69%
Howe	92%
Anderson	96%
Wolley	88%
Goerz	74%

Tippecanoe Typing is suffering from financial difficulties and needs to cut back on its staff. Using READ, DATA and a loop, have the computer print notices of dismissal for any employee whose production performance is below 75%.

3 COMPUTER GAMES

This chapter introduces material which we hope will be interesting, practical, and entertaining. In fact, the emphasis is placed on employing APPLESOFT to involve the user in computer games, easily the best and most enjoyable way to learn computer programming.

RND

In many computer simulations involving laboratory experiments, problems in social science, and a variety of games the process of generating random numbers becomes essential. RND will cause the computer to produce a random number between 0 and 1. For example,

```
20 R = RND (1)
```

assigns a random number to the variable R.

PROGRAM 3.1

This program will produce ten random numbers between 0 and 1.

```
10  FOR X = 1 TO 10
20 R =  RND (1)
30  PRINT R
40  NEXT X

]RUN
.776733737
.479674134
.261322896
.896396026
.185497918
.490230353
.4637721
.363803188
.698794455
.317724406

]
```

It is not necessary to put a 1 inside the parentheses next to RND. In fact, the number within the parentheses will not affect the result so long as it is a positive integer.

INT

The statement A=INT(X) makes A the largest integer that is not greater than X. Note that this function does not round off a positive number, but simply truncates its decimals. In the case of a negative number, it takes the next lower integer. For example:

INT (3.7640) = 3   INT (5.9) = 5
INT (-1.7) = -2   INT (-3.01) = -4

The process of rounding off a number to the nearest integer is done by writing A= INT(X+.5). For example:

If X = 3.4, then 3.4 + .5 = 3.9, and INT(3.9) =3.
If X = 3.6, then 3.6 + .5 = 4.1, and INT(4.1) =4.

```
]PRINT INT(3.6+.5)
4

]PRINT INT(3.1+.5)
3

]PRINT INT(3.5+.5)
4

]
```

The INT function is also used to round off numbers to any desired number of decimal places. For example, INT(10*X + .5) /10 will round X to one decimal place. If X = 2.57, then (10*X + .5) = (25.7 + .5) = 26.2 and INT (26.2) = 26. If the 26 is then divided by 10 the result is 2.6, the correct rounded value. Furthermore, INT(100*X + .5) /100 rounds X to two decimal places and INT(1000*X + .5) /1000 to three places and so on. Rounding off a number to the nearest ten (e.g., 257 becomes 260) is accomplished by using INT(.1*X + .5) /.1. A general formula for rounding X to N decimal places is:

INT(10↑N*X+.5)/10↑N

PROGRAM 3.2

This program is a revision of Program 3.1 and it uses INT and RND to produce ten random integers in the range between 0 and 9.

```
10  FOR X = 1 TO 10
20 R =  INT (10 *  RND (1))
30  PRINT R;"  ";
40  NEXT X

]RUN
2  7  4  3  2  2  7  4  1  2
]
```

On line 20 the random number is multiplied by ten and is then changed to the proper integer. Note that line 20 would produce 0 if RND(1) were close to 0 and would produce 9 if RND(1) was close to 1.

The following equation may be used to generate a random integer in which N is the number of integers in the set with A the lowest integer.

20 R = INT (N * RND (1) + A)

To produce a set of random integers from 40 to 50, inclusive, use N = 11 and A = 40 in the new line 20 of Program 3.2.

```
]20 R=INT(11*RND(1)+40)

]RUN
43   40   46   40   41   47   48   50   42   50
]
```

PROGRAM 3.3

This game program selects a random number between 1 and 100 and then gives the player an unlimited number of chances to guess it. After each guess the computer informs the player whether the guess is too high, too low or correct.

```
10 R =  INT (100 *  RND (1) + 1)
20  INPUT "WHAT IS YOUR GUESS? ";G
30  IF G < R THEN 60
40  IF G = R THEN 70
50  PRINT "TOO HIGH": GOTO 20
60  PRINT "TOO LOW": GOTO 20
70  PRINT "THAT IS CORRECT!"

]RUN
WHAT IS YOUR GUESS? 50
TOO LOW
WHAT IS YOUR GUESS? 75
TOO LOW
WHAT IS YOUR GUESS? 83
TOO HIGH
WHAT IS YOUR GUESS? 79
TOO HIGH
WHAT IS YOUR GUESS? 77
TOO LOW
WHAT IS YOUR GUESS? 78
THAT IS CORRECT!
```

REVIEW

1. Write a program to produce 12 random numbers from 250 to 275, inclusive.

```
]RUN
261   253   267   252   270   256   257   254   275   258   258   250
]
```

2. Write a game program similar to Program 3.3 which picks a random number between 1 and 50, inclusive, and gives the player only five attempts to guess it.

```
]RUN
WHAT IS YOUR GUESS? 25
TOO HIGH
WHAT IS YOUR GUESS? 12
TOO HIGH
WHAT IS YOUR GUESS? 6
TOO LOW
WHAT IS YOUR GUESS? 9
TOO HIGH
WHAT IS YOUR GUESS? 8
TOO HIGH
YOU HAVE MADE TOO MANY MISTAKES.
THE NUMBER WAS 7
```

Summation

If the user had decided to keep score for the number guessing game of Program 3.3, some technique would have had to be devised to keep count of the number of guesses taken. One possible technique is to use a summation statement of the form:

30 A=A+1

The statement A=A+1 makes no sense in mathematics since A can equal A but not A+1. The computer, however, interprets the equal sign to mean "is replaced by" rather than "equal to", and each time it encounters line 30 above, it takes the present value of A, adds 1 to it and makes that sum the new value of A.

PROGRAM 3.4

This program demonstrates how the summation statement works by printing the values of A until the program is halted with a CTRL-C.

```
10 A = A + 1
20  PRINT A;"   ";
30  GOTO 10

]RUN
1  2  3  4  5  6  7  8  9  10  11  12  13  14  15  16
BREAK IN 20
]
```

Should we replace line 10 with

10 A=A+5

then 5 will be added to A each time the statement is encountered.

```
]10 A=A+5

]RUN
5  10  15  20  25  30  35  40  45  50  55  60  65  70  75  80
BREAK IN 20
]
```

In this problem the initial value of A is zero for both runs. This is true because the APPLE sets any undefined numeric variable to zero at the start of a run.

PROGRAM 3.5

Here, Program 3.3 has been modified to record the number of turns required to guess the random number. In this case the variable T acts as a counter, increasing in value by 1 after each guess.

```
10 R =  INT (100 *  RND (1) + 1)
20  INPUT "WHAT IS YOUR GUESS? ";G
25 T = T + 1
30  IF G < R THEN 60
40  IF R = G THEN 70
50  PRINT "TOO HIGH": GOTO 20
60  PRINT "TOO LOW": GOTO 20
70  PRINT "THAT IS CORRECT!"
80  PRINT "THAT TOOK ";T;" TRIES."

]RUN
WHAT IS YOUR GUESS? 50
TOO LOW
WHAT IS YOUR GUESS? 75
TOO HIGH
WHAT IS YOUR GUESS? 62
THAT IS CORRECT!
THAT TOOK 3 TRIES.

]
```

Rounding Errors

Because the computer has a finite capacity, any numerical computations involving infinitely repeating decimals cannot be accurate. A base 10 example is 1/3 = .3333 . . . , which the computer truncates to a limited number of digits. Since the computer uses binary numbers (base 2), any fraction whose denominator is not an integral power of 2 (e.g., 2, 4,

8, 16) will be an infinitely repeating decimal and therefore be truncated by the computer. In Chapter Nine binary numbers are treated in greater detail.

PROGRAM 3.6

This program illustrates the processes of summation and rounding error.

```
10   FOR X = 1 TO 1500
20 A = A + 1 / 2
30 B = B + 1 / 3
40   NEXT X
50   PRINT "A=";A
60   PRINT "B=";B

]RUN
A=750
B=500.000023
```

The final value of A is the result of adding 1/2, 1500 times and it comes out exactly 750. B, however, which is the result of adding 1/3, 1500 times does not come out exactly 500 because of the rounding error.

REVIEW

3. Select 50 random integers between 0 and 9, inclusive, and have the computer tell how many of the numbers were from 0-4 and how many were from 5-9.

```
]RUN
(0-4): 27
(5-9): 23

]
```

4. Input ten numbers from the keyboard, and have the computer tell how many are odd and how many are even.

```
]RUN
?24
?85
?64
?34
?8
?64
?75
?5
?76
?76

7 EVEN          3 ODD

]
```

PRINT TAB

The PRINT TAB statement provides an easy way to format output. It allows the programmer to begin portions of the printout at specified locations. The left edge of the screen is TAB(1), and the right edge of the screen is TAB(40). The printing of information at TAB positions 13, 25 and 32 is accomplished by:

```
10  PRINT  TAB( 13);"THIS"; TAB( 25);"IS"; TAB( 32);"TAB"

]RUN
            THIS        IS      TAB

]
```

Here it is important to use semicolons (;) in each instance after the TAB parentheses.

PROGRAM 3.7

The substitution of variables for the numbers in the TAB parentheses is permissible provided these variables have been previously assigned values.

```
10  READ X,Y,Z
20  DATA  13,25,32
30  PRINT  TAB( X);"THIS"; TAB( Y);"IS"; TAB( Z);"TAB"

]RUN
            THIS        IS      TAB

]
```

PROGRAM 3.8

This program will draw a rectangle on the screen.

```
10  PRINT  TAB( 5);"*******"
20  FOR X = 1 TO 5
30  PRINT  TAB( 5);"*"; TAB( 11);"*"
40  NEXT X
50  PRINT  TAB( 5);"*******"

]RUN
    *******
    *     *
    *     *
    *     *
    *     *
    *     *
    *******

]
```

Note that the PRINT TAB statement does not move the cursor to the left, but only to the right. If a TAB position is specified which is to the left of the current TAB position, the cursor will remain where it is and the printing will proceed from there.

```
10  PRINT  TAB( 10);"##"; TAB( 15);"##"
20  PRINT  TAB( 15);"##"; TAB( 10);"##"

]RUN
         ##   ##
              ####

]
```

HTAB, VTAB, and HOME

HTAB and VTAB are used without PRINT statements to move the cursor around the screen. VTAB moves the cursor vertically on the screen. VTAB(1) refers to the top of the screen, and VTAB(24) moves the cursor to the bottom of the screen. Unlike TAB, HTAB can move the cursor to the left as well as the right. HTAB(1) will place the cursor at the left edge of the screen, and HTAB(40) will place the cursor at the right edge of the screen. HOME will erase the screen and place the cursor in the upper left-hand corner of the screen.

PROGRAM 3.9

This program will randomly place 20 asterisks or "stars" on the video screen.

```
5   HOME
10   FOR N = 1 TO 20
20 X =  INT (40 *  RND (1) + 1)
30 Y =  INT (24 *  RND (1) + 1)
40   HTAB (X)
50   VTAB (Y)
60   PRINT "*"
70   NEXT N

]RUN

                   *         *
        *     *          **      *

         *             *

        *        *          **
*       *               *
      *     *                     *
                           *
```

FLASH, INVERSE, and NORMAL

The FLASH command causes anything that the computer prints to flash from white on black, or to black on white in a manner similar to the flashing cursor. INVERSE causes anything that the computer prints to appear as black on white. NORMAL will cancel a FLASH or INVERSE command. FLASH and INVERSE will only affect output from the computer, and not characters which appear on the screen when they are entered at the keyboard.

PROGRAM 3.10

This program is a very simple version of STAR WARS. The computer randomly places a "star" on the screen and asks the player for its X and Y coordinates. If the player chooses the wrong coordinates, the computer flashes the message MISSED and indicates whether each coordinate has been given a guess which is either too high or too low. When the star is hit, the message HIT is flashed. The player starts with a score of 100 points and loses 5 points for each miss. The score is given at the end of the game.

Type the program into the APPLE, and try to play it. By expanding and refining the program, you can make it considerably more sophisticated and intricate.

```
10 A = 100
20  HOME
30 X =  INT (40 *  RND (1) + 1)
40 Y =  INT (24 *  RND (1) + 1)
50  HTAB (X)
60  VTAB (Y)
70  PRINT "*"
80  INPUT "WHAT IS THE X-COORDINATE? ";X1
90  INPUT "WHAT IS THE Y-COORDINATE ?";Y1
100  IF X = X1 AND Y = Y1 THEN 200
110  IF X1 > X THEN  PRINT "X-COORDINATE IS TOO HIGH"
120  IF Y1 > Y THEN  PRINT "Y-COORDINATE IS TOO HIGH"
130  IF X1 < X THEN  PRINT "X-COORDINATE IS TOO LOW"
140  IF Y1 < Y THEN  PRINT "Y-COORDINATE IS TOO LOW"
150 A = A - 10
160  FLASH
170  PRINT "MISSED"
180  NORMAL
190  GOTO 80
200  FLASH
210  PRINT "HIT"
220  NORMAL
230  PRINT "YOUR SCORE IS ";A
```

EXERCISES

PART A

1. Generate ten random numbers between 0 and 1, but print only those which are greater then 0.5.

2. Generate three random numbers between 0 and 1, and print their sum.

3. Input a number (N). Print it only if it is an integer. (Hint: compare N and INT(N)).

4. Allow a user to guess a random integer between -3 and 4, inclusive. Print whether the guess was correct or not. If the guess was wrong, the correct value is also to be printed.

5. Determine randomly how many coins you find on the street. You are to find from 2 to 5 nickels, 1 to 4 dimes, and 0 to 3 quarters. Lunch costs 99 cents. The program is to report the amount that you found and whether you are able to buy lunch with it.

6. Input an integer (N), and print the sum of N random numbers between 0 and 1. Also print N/2 for comparison with the sum.

7. A child puts pennies into a piggy bank once each week for four weeks. The bank already contains 11 pennies in it when the child first receives it. Write a program to allow pennies to be added each week and to print the dollar value of the bank's contents after each addition.

8. Have the computer produce the following output.

```
]RUN
1234567890123456789012345678901234567890

*       9     ?     -       !   )      *
```

9. Use HTAB and VTAB to draw a straight diagonal line (composed of asterisks) starting at the upper left hand corner and moving one space over for each space down until the line hits the bottom of the screen.

10. Put a flashing notice on the screen which advertises Uncle Bill's whamburgers for $0.59.

```
]RUN
-----------------------------
!                           !
! TODAY ONLY!               !
!        UNCLE BILL'S       !
!        WHAMBURGERS        !
!              ONLY 0.59    !
!                           !
-----------------------------
```

PART B

11. Les Brains wrote both of the following programs but has forgotten what their output is. Determine the output, and check your answer by running the program.

(a)

```
10  FOR Z = 1 TO 4
20  PRINT  TAB( Z);Z
30  NEXT Z
40  FOR Y = 1 TO 4
50  PRINT  TAB( Y),Y
60  NEXT Y
```

(b)

```
10 G = 123.456
20  PRINT  INT (10 * G) / 10, INT (10 * G + .5) / 10
30  PRINT  INT (100 * G) / 100, INT (100 * G + .5) / 100
```

12. Write a program that generates 12 random integers between 8 and 25, inclusive, and prints them on the same line. The output should be similar to the following:

13 17 12 22 25 8 17 19 11 21 23 18

13. Make a chart showing in their correct order the values taken by the variables X and Y. Circle those values that are printed by the computer. Check by running the program.

```
10  FOR X = 1 TO 3
15  READ Y
20  IF Y > 0 THEN 35
25 Y = Y + X
30  IF X = 2 THEN Y = Y - 1: GOTO 40
35  PRINT X,Y
40  NEXT X
45  DATA  5,0,-1
```

14. (a) Determine a possible output for the program below.
(b) Rewrite the program so that the message LEARN THE MULTIPLICATION TABLE is printed if three wrong answers are given.
(c) Rewrite the program so that five different questions are asked and the message NICE GOING, HOTSHOT is printed if all five questions are answered correctly.

```
10  HOME : VTAB (10)
20 A =  INT (10 *  RND (1) + 1)
30 B =  INT (10 *  RND (1) + 1)
40  PRINT  TAB( 12);A;" * ";B;" = ";
50  INPUT C
60  IF C = A * B THEN 90
70  PRINT "YOU ARE WRONG. TRY AGAIN."
80  GOTO 40
90  PRINT  TAB( 12);
100  FLASH : PRINT "CORRECT": NORMAL
```

15. Write a program that contains one FOR . . . NEXT loop which finds the sum of all the odd integers from 13 to 147, inclusive. The output should be as follows:

THE SUM = 5440

16. Suzy Fowlup, one of the slower members of the computing class, wrote the following program. It allows the user to enter at the keyboard any integer greater than 1 and to have the computer tell the user whether or not the integer is prime. A prime number is an integer that contains only itself and 1 as factors. The computer tests the integer by repeatedly dividing it by integers smaller than itself but larger than 1 and checking whether the quotient is whole. If so, the integer entered by the user is not prime. The program contains three errors. Find them, rewrite the program, and run it. The output should look like this:

```
]RUN
INTEGER > 1, PLEASE? 12
THAT INTEGER IS NOT PRIME.

]RUN
INTEGER > 1, PLEASE? 17
THAT INTEGER IS PRIME.
```

```
20  READ "INTEGER > 1, PLEASE? ";N
30  FOR X = 2 TO N - 1
40  IF N / X =  INT (N / X) THEN 70
50  NEXT N
60  PRINT "THAT INTEGER IS PRIME."
70  PRINT "THAT INTEGER IS NOT PRIME."
```

17. Generate 1000 random integers between 1 and 9, inclusive, and print how many were even and how many were odd. The output should be similar to the following:

```
THERE WERE 572 ODD INTEGERS
THERE WERE 428 EVEN INTEGERS
```

18. Write a program that allows the user and computer to alternately select integers between 3 and 12, inclusive, keep a sum of all the integers selected, and declare the winner to be the one who selects that integer which makes the sum greater than 100. Have the program ask the user if he would like to proceed first or second.

19. A bank pays interest once a year at a yearly rate of 5%. A man deposits $1000 on January 1, 1980 and wishes to leave it there to accrue interest until the balance is at least $2000. Compute the balance on Jan. 1 of each year, starting with 1981 and ending in the year when the balance exceeds $2000. The output should resemble the following:

```
DATE              BALANCE
JAN 1, 1981       $1050
JAN 1, 1982       $1102.5
   ...               ...
   ...               ...
   ...            $1979.93
   ...            $2078.93
```

20. Input a positive integer N, and print all positive integers that are factors of N. The output should resemble the following:

```
]RUN
A POSITIVE INTEGER, PLEASE? 1.4
YOUR NUMBER WAS NOT AN INTEGER.
A POSITIVE INTEGER, PLEASE? 12
1  2  3  4  6  12
]
```

21. Print the radius (cm.) of a sphere, given its volume (cm.^{3}). Round off the results to the nearest hundredth.

DATA: 690, 720, 460, 620
Note: Volume = $(4/3)(\pi)R^3$, where $\pi = 3.14159$

22. (a) Print twenty random integers between 0 and 100, inclusive.
(b) Change the program so that sixty percent of the twenty integers printed will be less than 25.

23. Write a program that will produce the following triangle. The figure is centered on TAB(15).

```
]RUN
              *
             * *
            *   *
           *     *
          *       *
         *         *
        *************
```

24. Modify the answer to Exercise 23 so that every other line in the triangle is flashing.

25. Using HTAB and VTAB, write a program that will draw a football made of asterisks. (Hint: use the equation of a circle.)

```
       *
   *       *
  *         *
 *           *
 *           *
 *           *
 *           *
 *           *
  *         *
   *       *
       *
```

26. (a) Have the Apple print the dart board pictured below, and have it fire ten random shots, using an asterisk to indicate the spot hit. The top of the outer square is on line 3 and its two vertical sides are at TAB(10) and TAB(30).

```
]RUN
          ---------------------
          !                   !
          !                   !
          !                   !
          !                   !
          !        -----      !
          !        !   !      !
          !        !   !      !
          !        !   !      !
          !        !   !      !
          !        -----      !
          !                   !
          !                   !
          !                   !
          !                   !
          ---------------------
```

(b) Rewrite program (a) to give the score at the end of a game. A hit in the center square is worth 10 points, the outer square 4 points, and the region outside both -1 points.

(c) Rewrite program (b) so that all hits inside either square flash.

27. Have the computer randomly select a number of quarters (from 0 to 7), dimes (from 0 to 4), and pennies (from 0 to 9) and print the exact number of coins and their total value. The user has ten chances to determine how many quarters, dimes and pennies were selected.

28. Using only one print statement, produce the following output. The names are spaced 10 spaces from the beginning of one name to the beginning of the next and down one line.

```
]RUN
BAUER
          BEDFORD
                    BENSEL
BURNS
          COMPTON
                    COOK
HARWOOD
          HENRY
                    STOKES

]
```

29. Luke Skywalker needs a simple simulator for his APPLE so that he can train before his next battle against the Empire. Help Luke by writing a simple Star Wars game. Have the computer print two asterisks at random positions on the screen. Luke has ten chances to guess the X and Y coordinates of the two enemy asterisks or the Rebellion will fail. The computer should flash a message at the end of the game stating the outcome. Use HTAB and VTAB to position the input line every time so that the enemy asterisks are not pushed off the top of the screen during the course of the game.

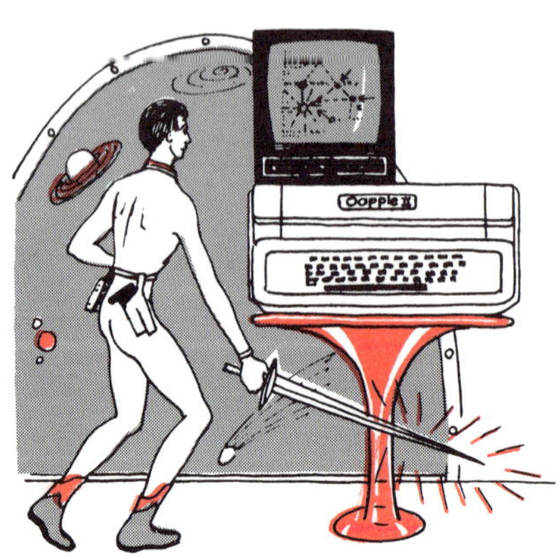

4 NESTED LOOPS AND SUBSCRIPTED VARIABLES

We have previously observed that the FOR . . . TO . . . STEP, NEXT statements set up loops. This chapter proceeds further by showing how to combine two or more FOR . . . NEXT loops in such a way as to place some entirely inside others. In such an arrangement, the loops are called nested loops.

The second part of the chapter deals with subscripted variables which use a fixed variable name in conjunction with a variable subscript (e.g., A(I)), where A is fixed and I varies. This technique enables a program to deal conveniently with a large amount of data. Subscripted variables usually employ FOR . . . NEXT loops to generate the values for the subscripts.

Nested FOR . . . NEXT Loops

FOR . . . NEXT loops can be used in groups of two or more. At this point we introduce the concept of nested FOR . . . NEXT loops, which are simply loops within loops. For example,

```
10   FOR X = 1 TO 20
20   FOR Y = 1 TO 5
30   NEXT Y
40   NEXT X
```

Since by definition nested loops must never cross, note that the Y loop is contained entirely within the X loop. For example, the following arrangement is not permissible.

```
10   FOR X = 1 TO 20
20   FOR A = 1 TO 5
40   NEXT X
50   NEXT A
```

Running this program will result in the error message:

?NEXT WITHOUT FOR ERROR IN 50

PROGRAM 4.1

This program uses nested loops to print a portion of the multiplication table.

```
10   FOR X = 1 TO 5
20   FOR Y = 1 TO 3
30   PRINT X;"*";Y;"=";X * Y,
40   NEXT Y
50   NEXT X

]RUN
1*1=1              1*2=2              1*3=3
2*1=2              2*2=4              2*3=6
3*1=3              3*2=6              3*3=9
4*1=4              4*2=8              4*3=12
5*1=5              5*2=10             5*3=15
```

Line 10 establishes the X loop and starts X with the value 1. X will retain this value until it is changed to the value 2 by the execution of line 50. Line 50 is not executed, however, until the Y loop, lines 20-40, has run its entire course. X therefore retains the value 1 while Y changes from 1 to 2 to 3. When the Y loop has finished its cycle of three passes, line 50 changes X to 2. The program returns to line 20 and starts the Y loop at its initial value of 1. Whenever a program returns to a FOR . . . NEXT loop, the loop variable is reset to its initial value. Since this program does not return to line 10, the X loop is never reset. Notice that Y will take on its values of 1, 2, and 3 five times.

REVIEW

1. Use nested loops to produce the following output. The outer loop variable (X) runs from 20 to 24, and the inner loop variable (Y) runs from 1 to 3.

```
X=20
Y=1                Y=2                Y=3
X=21
Y=1                Y=2                Y=3
X=22
Y=1                Y=2                Y=3
X=23
Y=1                Y=2                Y=3
X=24
Y=1                Y=2                Y=3
```

TRACE and NOTRACE

The TRACE command helps to clarify the concept of nested loops. When the TRACE command is used, the computer prints every line number as it is executed preceded by the symbol "#". The NOTRACE command stops the printing of line numbers.

PROGRAM 4.2

This program illustrates the use of TRACE and NOTRACE.

```
10  TRACE
20  FOR X = 1 TO 10
30 Z = Z + 2
40  NEXT X
50  PRINT Z
60  NOTRACE

]RUN
#20 #30 #40 #30 #40 #30 #40 #30 #40 #30 #40 #30
 #40 #30 #40 #30 #40 #30 #40 #30 #40 #50 20
#60
```

Note the long succession of "#30 #40 #30 . . ." This comes from the ten executions of the FOR . . . NEXT loop. Remember that the NEXT statement returns the program to the statement directly after the FOR . . . TO statement.

Nested loops are especially useful when a problem is solved by trial-and-error. In this method, though many results are calculated, only solutions are retained.

PROGRAM 4.3

This program calculates and prints all possible combinations of coins that add up to fifty cents, using quarters, dimes, and nickels.

```
10  PRINT "QUARTERS","DIMES","NICKELS"
20  FOR Q = 0 TO 2
30  FOR D = 0 TO 5
40  FOR N = 0 TO 10
50  IF Q * 25 + D * 10 + N * 5 = 50 THEN  PRINT Q,D,N
60  NEXT N
70  NEXT D
80  NEXT Q

]RUN
QUARTERS          DIMES             NICKELS
0                 0                 10
0                 1                 8
0                 2                 6
0                 3                 4
0                 4                 2
0                 5                 0
1                 0                 5
1                 1                 3
1                 2                 1
2                 0                 0
```

Q represents the number of quarters, D the number of dimes, and N the number of nickels. There may be anywhere from 0 to 2 quarters in a combination because 2 quarters equals fifty cents. Similarly, there may be anywhere from 0 to 5 dimes and from 0 to 10 nickels. Using three nested loops, *every* possible combination that *might* work is checked at line 50.

The Need for Subscripted Variables

PROGRAM 4.4

The following program generates ten random numbers between 1 and 20. Notice that both 20 and 17 are repeated in the output because the program does nothing to prevent repetition.

```
10  FOR X = 1 TO 10
20 Y =  INT (20 *  RND (1) + 1)
30  PRINT Y;" ";
40  NEXT X

]RUN
5 14 1 16 20 13 20 11 17 17
```

In this program every time a new value is assigned to Y it replaces the previous value for Y. Since the previous values of Y are no longer available, it is impossible to prevent repetition by comparing the old with the new value. If the box analogy is used here, the first two cycles of Program 4.4 would appear as:

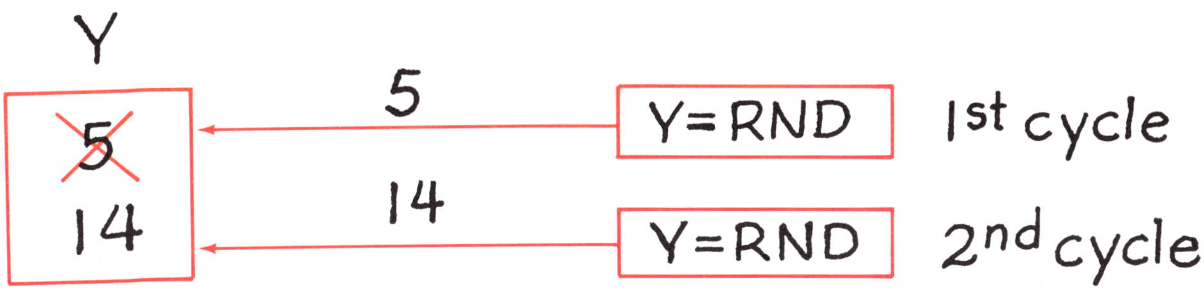

PROGRAM 4.5

This program prints four random numbers between 1 and 20 without allowing repetition. The technique could be expanded to have the program choose 10 numbers if the user were dogged enough to type the program lines required.

```
10 Y1 =  INT (20 *  RND (1) + 1)
20  PRINT Y1;" ";
30 Y2 =  INT (20 *  RND (1) + 1)
40  IF Y2 = Y1 THEN 30
50  PRINT Y2;" ";
60 Y3 =  INT (20 *  RND (1) + 1)
70  IF Y3 = Y2 OR Y3 = Y1 THEN 60
80  PRINT Y3;" ";
90 Y4 =  INT (20 *  RND (1) + 1)
100  IF Y4 = Y3 OR Y4 = Y2 OR Y4 = Y1 THEN 90
110  PRINT Y4

]RUN
6 17 3 12
```

The similarity between the three sets of lines 30-50, 60-80, and 90-110 is obvious. In each set the first line selects a random number between 1 and 20. The second line checks to see if the number is a repetition of a number previously chosen. If this be the case, then execution goes back to the first line in the set so that another number may be chosen. Finally, the third line prints the random number. The use of subscripted variables will eliminate this redundancy.

Single Subscripted Variables

In mathematics a set of single subscripted numeric variables (e.g., x_1, x_2, x_3, and x_4) is symbolized by a letter and a subscript which is written below the line. On the APPLE the same set of subscripted variables would be referred to as X(1), X(2), X(3), and X(4), where the integer enclosed in parentheses is the subscript.

The name for a set of single subscripted numeric variables consists of one of the usual numeric names, followed by the parenthesized subscript. For example, A(1), B2(17), and X(I) are all legal names (provided that I is a positive integer). Similarly, single subscripted string variable names such as Z$(5), Y1$(20), and M$(500) are acceptable.

The subscripted variable L(1) is *not* the same as a variable L1. Furthermore, the subscript is a part of the variable name and must not be confused with the value of the variable. For example, in the statement L(5) = 32, the subscript is 5, but the value of the variable is 32.

PROGRAM 4.6

This program illustrates the difference between the subscript and the value of a subscripted variable.

```
10 L(1) = 7
20 L(2) = 5
30 L(3) = 4
40   PRINT L(1),L(2),L(3)
50   PRINT L(1 + 2)
60   PRINT L(1) + L(2)
70 X = 2
80   PRINT L(X)

]RUN
7                5                4
4
12
5
```

Lines 10 through 30 set the values of L(1) through L(3) as follows:

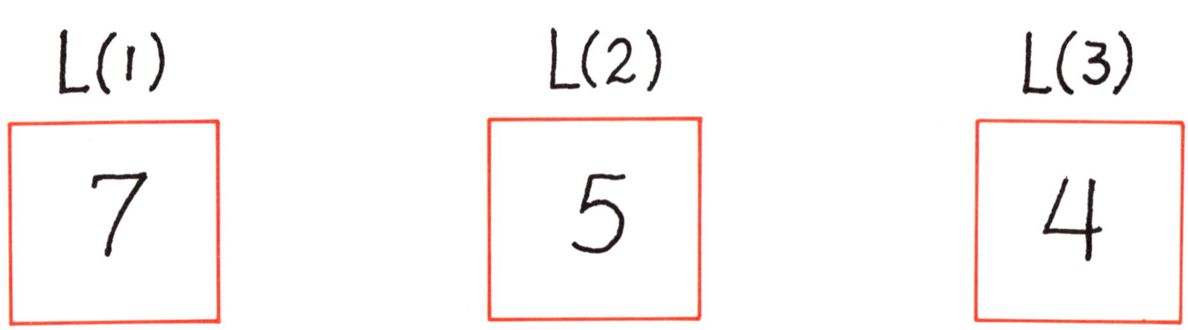

Lines 50 and 60 point out the difference between adding two subscripts and adding the values of two variables. L(1 + 2) is L(3) and has a value of 4. L(1) + L(2) calls for the values 7 and 5 to be added, thus producing a total of 12. Since the subscript equals 2, line 80 prints a value of 5.

PROGRAM 4.7

Like Program 4.4, this present program selects 10 random numbers between 1 and 20 and makes no attempt to prevent repetition. Yet unlike Program 4.4, it stores the numbers by using subscripted variables.

```
10  FOR X = 1 TO 10
20 Y(X) =  INT (20 *  RND (1) + 1)
30  NEXT X
40  PRINT "ALL OF THE NUMBERS HAVE BEEN STORED."
45  PRINT
50  FOR X = 1 TO 10
60  PRINT "BOX # ";X;" HAS A ";Y(X);" STORED IN IT."
70  NEXT X

]RUN
ALL OF THE NUMBERS HAVE BEEN STORED.

BOX # 1 HAS A 15 STORED IN IT.
BOX # 2 HAS A 6 STORED IN IT.
BOX # 3 HAS A 6 STORED IN IT.
BOX # 4 HAS A 11 STORED IN IT.
BOX # 5 HAS A 16 STORED IN IT.
BOX # 6 HAS A 2 STORED IN IT.
BOX # 7 HAS A 2 STORED IN IT.
BOX # 8 HAS A 18 STORED IN IT.
BOX # 9 HAS A 19 STORED IN IT.
BOX # 10 HAS A 11 STORED IN IT.
```

The program has two loops which are not nested but rather proceed one after the other. Each loop is executed 10 times. In the first loop at line 20 a random number is chosen and is stored in one of the subscripted Y variables. The first time through this loop (X = 1), a random number is stored in Y(1); the second time (X = 2), a new number is stored in Y(2) and so on 10 times. After the above run of this program, the Y boxes had contents as follows.

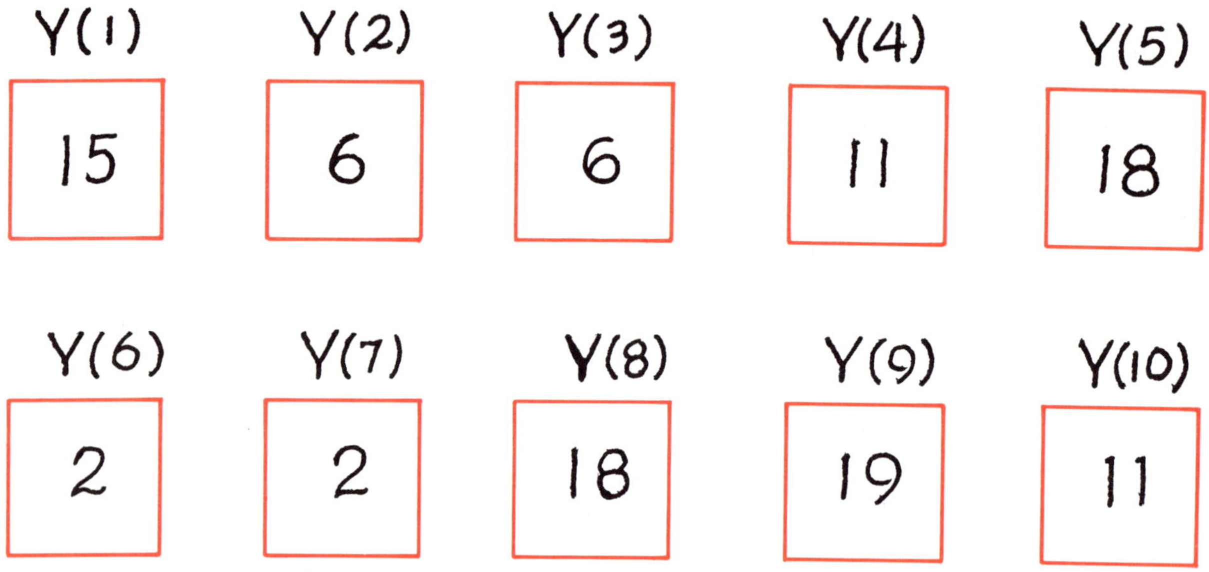

The second loop (lines 50 through 70) prints the stored contents of the boxes.

The ability to store numbers will allow a new program to be written to choose 10 random numbers without repetition. By recognizing if the next chosen number equals any of those previously stored, the program determines whether to accept the next number or to make another selection.

PROGRAM 4.8

This program uses nested loops and subscripted variables to pick 10 random numbers between 1 and 20 without repetition.

```
10  FOR X = 1 TO 10
20 Y(X) =  INT (20 *  RND (1) + 1)
30  IF X = 1 THEN 70
40  FOR Q = 1 TO X - 1
50  IF Y(X) = Y(Q) THEN 20
60  NEXT Q
70  PRINT Y(X);" ";
80  NEXT X

]RUN
12 20 1 10 9 6 15 14 3 11
```

Line 20 selects a random number from 1 to 20 and stores it. Since Y(1) cannot be a repeated number, line 30 is included to ensure that Y(1) will be printed immediately. Lines 40 to 60 constitute a nested loop which determines if a number just chosen (Y(X)) is equal to any of the previously chosen numbers (Y(1) to Y(X-1)). The X-1 in line 40 ensures that Y(X) is not rejected by being checked against itself. If X, rather than X-1, were used, then Q would eventually equal X. Line 50 would determine that Y(X) was a repeated number when Q equalled X and would mistakenly return to line 20.

There is an additional reason for including line 30. If it were deleted, then when both X and Q were equal to 1, line 50 would transfer control back to line 20 thus, requiring a CTRL-C command to stop the run.

PROGRAM 4.9

The following program will randomly read a list of 5 names into a subscripted string variable N$(Y), without repeating any of the names.

```
10  FOR X = 1 TO 5
20 Y =  INT ( RND (1) * 5 + 1)
30  IF N$(Y) <  > "" THEN 20
40  READ N$(Y)
50  NEXT X
60  FOR Z = 1 TO 5
70  PRINT N$(Z)
80  NEXT Z
90  DATA  FRED,SAM,EDGAR,GERTRUDE,MILDRED

]RUN
FRED
MILDRED
GERTRUDE
EDGAR
SAM

]RUN
MILDRED
SAM
GERTRUDE
FRED
EDGAR
```

This program reads the names in the DATA statement in the order of occurrence, but randomly places them in the boxes N$(1) to N$(5). Repetition is avoided by checking each new box as it is selected to discover whether it contains a name. If it is full, a new box is tried by selecting a new random number. On line 30 the consecutive double quotes ("") refer to the box being empty. Unassigned subscripted string variables contain an empty space, which is represented on the computer by ("").

REVIEW

2. Using subscripted variables, write a program in which 3 numbers are input. Then have the computer type them back in reverse order.

```
]RUN
?4
?6
?1

1
6
4
```

3. Six words are to be entered from the keyboard. Have the computer randomly select and print four of the words as a "sentence" (which may not make sense). Repetition of words is allowed.

```
]RUN
?JACK
?AND
?JILL
?RAN
?AWAY
?SCREAMING
JACK SCREAMING AWAY AWAY .
```

4. Rewrite the program of the preceding exercise, not allowing repetition.

```
]RUN
?JACK
?AND
?JILL
?RAN
?AWAY
?HAPPILY
AWAY JILL JACK HAPPILY .
```

DIM

Whenever the highest subscript of a subscripted variable exceeds 10, the computer must be informed. The DIM (dimension) statement is used to direct the computer to open enough boxes in its memory to accommodate the anticipated input. Program 4.9 could store 100 names by making the appropriate changes in several lines and by adding the line

```
5 DIM N$(100)
```

If the ages of the people were also to be stored, a numeric subscripted variable would have to be added and the DIM statement modified.

```
5 DIM N$(100), A(100)
```

It is possible to request more space (i.e. boxes) in memory than the computer can supply. This results in the error message:

```
?OUT OF MEMORY ERROR
```

Though it is possible to have several DIM statements in a program, each subscripted variable may only be dimensioned once. Having two DIM statements for the same variable or having the same DIM statement executed more than once will result in the error message:

```
?REDIM'D ARRAY ERROR
```

Double Subcripted Variables

APPLESOFT can also use double subscripts to name a variable. This is similar to single subscripting except for the fact that integers separated by commas must be enclosed in parentheses. For example,

```
A(1,5)     B3(7,3)     C$(4,9)
```

are all double subscripted variables. The computer reserves space in memory for a double subscripted variable by placing them in rows and columns, rather than in a single column (as is the case with a single subscripted variable). This procedure provides a convenient technique for dealing with problems in which the data is two-dimensional in nature, such as the location of seats in a theater.

To understand more clearly how the double subscripted variable operates, the box analogy is again helpful. The first integer in the subscript identifies the row and the second the column in which the variable is located. For example, A(2,3) is located at the second row, third column.

	Col.1	Col.2	Col.3	Col.4
Row 1	A(1,1)	A(1,2)	A(1,3)	A(1,4)
Row 2	A(2,1)	A(2,2)	A(2,3)	A(2,4)
Row 3	A(3,1)	A(3,2)	A(3,3)	A(3,4)

PROGRAM 4.10

A classroom has 5 rows of seats with 3 seats to a row. The following program randomly assigns a class of 14 students to seats, leaving one seat empty.

```
10  DIM N$(5,3)
20  FOR X = 1 TO 14
30  READ A$
40 R =  INT ( RND (1) * 5 + 1)
50 C =  INT ( RND (1) * 3 + 1)
60  IF N$(R,C) <  > "" THEN 40
70 N$(R,C) = A$
75  NEXT X
80  FOR R1 = 1 TO 5
90  FOR C1 = 1 TO 3
100  IF N$(R1,C1) = "" THEN  PRINT "EMPTY",: GOTO 120
110  PRINT N$(R1,C1),
120  NEXT C1
130  NEXT R1
140 DATA  ELLIOT,JEFF,DAVE,MATT,CLAIR
150 DATA  MIKE,LIZA,ROB,LESTER,JOHN
160 DATA  ANNE,WENDELL,JENNY,MARGOT
```

```
]RUN
LESTER          MIKE            EMPTY
DAVE            MARGOT          JEFF
JENNY           ROB             ELLIOT
MATT            JOHN            ANNE
WENDELL         CLAIR           LIZA
```

APPLESOFT also allows 3, 4, etc., all the way up to 88 dimensions in a subscripted variable (e.g.,DIM A(5,5,4,7,2,10,9). The more numbers there are inside the DIM statement, however, the smaller they must be. This is because the APPLE has only a limited number of boxes in its memory.

REVIEW

5. Six numbers are to be input from the keyboard as X(I). These are subsequently to be printed in a vertical column, and then a second time, closely spaced on a single line.

```
]RUN
?23
?67
?123
?37
?81
?376
23
67
123
37
81
376

23 67 123 37 81 376
```

6. Use the double subscripted variable X$(I,J) for which the row variable I runs from 1 to 5 and the column variable J from 1 to 3. Enter the letters A, B, C as the first row, D, E, F as the second, up to M, N, O as the fifth. Have the program print the following (making the rows become columns).

```
]RUN
A D G J M
B E H K N
C F I L O
```

Some Final Notes on Subscripted Variables

Subscripted string and numeric variables greatly enhance the programmer's ability to store and deal with large quantities of data within any one program run. It must be remembered, however, that if the program is run again, all of the stored data in the computer's memory is erased. This means that all of the boxes return either to blanks or to zeros at the start of the next run. Using STORE and RECALL, which are covered in Appendix A, it is possible to store permanently values of subscripted variables on cassettes. If disk drives are available, other commands appropriate for disk storage exist, and these are covered in Chapter 8.

Extended Variable Names

Previously, variable names have consisted of a single letter, possibly followed by a digit. As was pointed out in this chapter, these names may also be subscripted. Actually,

APPLESOFT variable names may be of any length. For example, ALPHABET, HAROLD, SCARE and BLACKBEARD23 are all permissable APPLESOFT variable names. There are, however, drawbacks to these names. Nowhere in the name of a variable may any normal APPLESOFT key word occur. For example, SCORE, FORTUNE, SAND and DIMWIT are all unacceptable variable names because they contain the words OR, FOR, AND, and DIM in them, respectively. Also, no matter how long the variable name may be, APPLESOFT only considers the first two characters. This means that the variable names XMIN and XMAX are considered the same because they both start with XM. Because of these drawbacks, it is recommended that extended variable names not be used except where they are useful in identifying what a variable represents.

EXERCISES

PART A

1. Have the computer print a rectangle consisting of eight lines of thirty asterisks each.

2. Show the output of the following program and check by running it. Rerun the program after removing line 50.

```
10  FOR I = 1 TO 5
20  FOR J = 1 TO 2 * I - 1
30  PRINT ".";
40  NEXT J
50  PRINT
60  NEXT I
```

3. Enter values of X(I) for I=1 to 6. Print the values of I and X(I) in two columns with I proceeding in the order 1, 3, 5, 2, 4, 6.

4. Enter 15 letters of the alphabet (not necessarily different), and print them in reverse order as a single block of letters.

5. Have the computer compute the values of A(I,J), where A(I,J)=3*I+J*J, I varies from 1 to 4, and J varies from 1 to 12. The user is to input a number N from 1 to 4 so that all values of A(N,J) can be printed.

6. Have the computer enter one letter of the alphabet for each member of A$(I,J), where I runs from 1 to 11 and J from 1 to 3. The letters are first to be printed in the form of

an 11 word sentence, with each word consisting of 3 letters. Then, the letters are to be printed again as a 3 word sentence, with each word consisting of 11 letters. The words may or may not make sense.

PART B

7. (a) Les Brains, who has forgotten where the computer is, needs to know the output for the following programs. Predict the output in each case, and check by running the program.

(a)
```
10   FOR L1 = 1 TO 3
20   FOR L2 = 5 TO 6
30   PRINT L1,L2
40   NEXT L2
50   NEXT L1
```

(b)
```
10   FOR X = 10 TO 15 STEP 2
20   FOR Y = 15 TO 10 STEP  - 2
30   IF Y = X THEN 99
40   IF X < Y THEN  PRINT X: GOTO 60
50   PRINT Y
60   NEXT Y
70   NEXT X
99   END
```

(c)
```
10   FOR S = 1 TO 10
20   READ A(S)
30   NEXT S
40   PRINT A(3),A(7),A(10)
50   DATA  23,12,45,2,67,34,89,17,2,35,70
```

8. Suzy Fowlup has done it again and has written another program that will not run properly. Assist her by correcting the program. The output should look like this:

```
]RUN
3                4
4                3
4                4
5                3
5                4
```

```
10  FOR A = 3,5
20  FOR B = 1,4
30  IF A * B <  = 10 GOTO 50
40 PRINYAB
50  NEXT A
60  NEXT B
```

9. The following program is designed to print the numbers in the DATA statement in decreasing order. However, there are some errors in the program. Correct and run the program to produce this output:

```
]RUN
40  37  27  27  16  9  8  5  2  1
]
```

```
10  FOR X = 40 TO 1
20  FOR Y = 1 TO 10
30  READ N
40  IF N = X THEN  PRINT N;"  ";
50  NEXT X
60  NEXT Y
70  DATA  5,27,37,16,27,8,2,40,1,9
```

10. What is the exact output for the following program?

```
10  READ B1,B2,B3,B4,B5,B6
20  FOR X = 1 TO 6: READ B(X): NEXT X
30  PRINT "B4=";B4;" BUT B(4)=";B(4)
40  PRINT B1 + B2 + B3,B(1) + B(2) + B(3),B(1 + 2 + 3)
50  DATA  3,7,4,1,9,12
51  DATA  14,2,9,19,10,11
```

11. The following program is designed to find random integers between 1 and 99, inclusive, until it encounters a duplicate. At that point it should print how many numbers it has found and then print all of them. However, there are a number of errors in the program. Correct them to produce output similar to:

```
]RUN
DUPLICATE AFTER 14 NUMBERS
70 98 79 29 71 75 10 85 76 7 25 83 89 76
]
```

```
20  FOR X = 1 TO 100
30 N(X) =  INT (99 *  RND (1) + 1)
40  FOR Y = 1 TO 100
50  IF N(X) <  > N(Y) THEN 70
60  PRINT "DUPLICATE AFTER ";X;"NUMBERS"
64  FOR Z = 1 TO X: PRINT N(X);"  ";: NEXT Z
70  NEXT Y
80  NEXT X
```

12. Write a program that reads the names, street addresses, towns, and zip codes of five people into subscripted variables N$(X), A$(X), T$(X), and Z$(X). The user enters a name, and the program prints the full name and address of that person. If the name is not there, have the program print PERSON NOT FOUND.

13. Find all sets of three integers, each between 1 and 10, inclusive, whose sum is 16. The integers within each group must be different from each other (e.g., 2,7,7, is not a permissible set). Each set should be printed exactly once (e.g., 2, 6, 8 and 6, 2, 8 should not both be printed). The output should resemble the following:

```
1  5  10
1  6  9
   ...
   ...
```

14. Stan's grocery store has 3 aisles. In each aisle there are 5 items. Write a program for Stan that will read 15 items into the subscripted variable I$(X,Y), dimensioned 3x5. Let his customers type in the item they want to buy, and be informed by the computer in which aisle to look.

15. Pick 20 random integers between 10 and 99, inclusive. Print the odd integers on one line and the even integers on the next line. The output should look like this:

```
]RUN
ODD INTEGERS: 29 , 77 , 27 , 43 , 45 , 43 , 21
, 67 , 53 , 75 ,
EVEN INTEGERS: 24 , 28 , 70 , 56 , 62 , 48 , 76
 , 32 , 96 , 54 ,
]
```

16. Find the average of four grades for each of five students. The output should give in columns on consecutive lines each student's name, four grades, and average. Each column should have a heading. The last student's average should be underlined and the class average printed below it in the same column.

```
]RUN
STUDENT #1 LESTER
ENTER FOUR GRADES:78,86,85,81
STUDENT #2 CATHY
ENTER FOUR GRADES:77,83,91,88
STUDENT #3 ROBERT
ENTER FOUR GRADES:82,81,77,81
STUDENT #4 TRICIA
ENTER FOUR GRADES:80,79,83,76
STUDENT #5 SHIRLY
ENTER FOUR GRADES:78,79,74,83
NAME           1    2    3    4     AVE.
LESTER         78   86   85   81    82.5
CATHY          77   83   91   88    84.75
ROBERT         82   81   77   81    80.25
TRICIA         80   79   83   76    79.5
SHIRLY         78   79   74   83    78.5
                                   ------
                                    81.1
```

17. Marcus Welby wants you to program the computer to keep track of his busy schedule. (a) Write a program to allow a patient to choose the day and time he or she wants to see the doctor. There are 5 days and 6 time slots for each day. If the desired slot is empty, the patient enters his or her name. If it is full, the program asks for another slot. (b) Add the steps needed to allow Dr. Welby to print his schedule for any particular day.

18. Susie Gossip has 3 skirts—red, green, and purple; 2 pairs of jeans—white and electric purple; 4 blouses—blue, pink, orange, and black; and 2 slightly tight sweaters—yellow and green. Have the Apple print a list of all possible combinations of the articles she can wear (e.g., red skirt and blue blouse, or white jeans and yellow sweater).

19. Write an extended version of the game high-low. In this game, the computer picks a secret random number between 1 and 100 and gives the player an unlimited number of chances to guess it. For each wrong guess the computer tells whether to guess higher or lower and stores the guess in a subscripted variable. If the player guesses the same number twice, the computer should produce the message WAKE UP! YOU GUESSED THAT NUMBER BEFORE.

20. Betty Bright has written the following two programs to sort data. Read the programs carefully and predict the output.

(a)
```
10   DIM A(10)
20   FOR B = 1 TO 10
30   READ A(B)
40   NEXT B
50   DATA  1,3,7,2,4,9,0,2,5,8
60   FOR C = 1 TO 10
70   FOR D = 0 TO C - 1
80   IF A(D) < A(C) THEN 100
90 E = A(D):A(D) = A(C):A(C) = E
100   NEXT D
110   NEXT C
120   FOR F = 1 TO 10
130   PRINT A(F)
140   NEXT F
```

```
(b) 10   DIM Q$(10)
    20   FOR M = 1 TO 10
    30   READ Q$(M)
    40   NEXT M
    50   DATA  LESTER,JULIE,ROBERT,SANDRA,JOHN
    60   DATA  KIM,DAVID,LISA,ERNIE,BECKY
    70   FOR R = 5 TO 10
    80   FOR Z = 5 TO R - 1
    90   IF Q$(Z) < Q$(R) THEN 110
    100  T$ = Q$(Z):Q$(Z) = Q$(R):Q$(R) = T$
    110   NEXT Z
    120   NEXT R
    130   FOR I = 10 TO 1 STEP  - 1
    140   PRINT Q$(I)
    150   NEXT I
```

21. The game Penny Pitch is common in amusement parks. Pennies are tossed onto a checkerboard on which numbers have been printed. By adding up the numbers in the squares on which the pennies fall, a score is accumulated. Write a program which simulates this game in which ten pennies are to be randomly pitched onto the board shown below.

1	1	1	1	1	1
1	2	2	2	2	1
1	2	3	3	2	1
1	2	3	3	2	1
1	2	2	2	2	1
1	1	1	1	1	1

Have the computer print the board with an X indicating where each penny has landed. Below is a sample run. Note that more than one penny can land in one square.

```
]RUN
 1   1   X   1   1   1

 1   2   2   2   2   1

 1   X   3   3   X   1

 X   X   3   X   X   1

 1   2   X   2   2   1

 1   1   X   X   1   1


          SCORE =17
```

22. Write a program that rolls two dice 1000 times and prints the number of times each different point total (2, 3, 4, 5, . . ., 12) appeared. The output should resemble the following:

```
]RUN
POINT TOTAL        TIMES APPEARED
    2                    33
    3                    61
    4                    106
   ...                   ...
    12                   35
```

23. Write a program which makes up 15 "words" (i.e. groups of letters, whether pronounceable or not) composed of from one to seven randomly chosen letters, and print them. (Hint: use addition of strings. For example if A$(2)="B" and A$(12)="L" then A$(2)+A$(12)="BL".)

24. Use the computer to play a modified game of Othello. Have it randomly fill an 8x8 subscripted string variable with X's and O's and print the array by row (horizontal) and column (vertical). Examples are below. The X's are for player 1, the O's for player 2. Have the program alternately ask the players for the row and column of the opponent's piece that should be flipped (changed from an X to an O or vice versa). All of the opponent's pieces along the horizontal or vertical line passing through the flipped

piece are also flipped. For example, if player 1 flipped the 0 at 2,2, board A would be changed to board B.

A
```
   1 2 3 4 5 6 7 8
 1 0 0 0 0 0 0 X 0
 2 0 0 0 X X 0 X X
 3 X 0 X 0 0 0 0 0
 4 X 0 X X 0 0 X 0
 5 X 0 X 0 X X 0 X
 6 0 X X 0 0 X X X
 7 0 X X X X 0 0 X
 8 0 0 0 X 0 0 0 X
```

B
```
   1 2 3 4 5 6 7 8
 1 0 X 0 0 0 0 X 0
 2 X X X X X X X X
 3 X X X 0 0 0 0 0
 4 X X X X 0 0 X 0
 5 X X X 0 X X 0 X
 6 0 X X 0 0 X X X
 7 0 X X X X 0 0 X
 8 0 X 0 X 0 0 0 X
```

5 MATHEMATICAL FUNCTIONS

This chapter covers the various mathematical functions that Applesoft can perform. The extent to which they can be useful to any individual depends on his or her mathematical background. Generally speaking, the functions presented here are primarily employed by mathematicians, scientists, and engineers.

SQR

The SQR function takes the square root of a number.

```
10 PRINT SQR(14)
```

The square root of a number N is defined as that value which, when multiplied by itself, gives N. For instance, the square root of 36 is 6 because 6x6=36.

PROGRAM 5.1

This program illustrates the square root function.

```
10   FOR X = 1 TO 4
20   PRINT "THE SQUARE ROOT OF ";X;" IS "; SQR (X)
30   NEXT X

]RUN
THE SQUARE ROOT OF 1 IS 1
THE SQUARE ROOT OF 2 IS 1.41421356
THE SQUARE ROOT OF 3 IS 1.73205081
THE SQUARE ROOT OF 4 IS 2
```

In the expression SQR(X), SQR is the function name and X is called the argument. With the SQR function, the argument may be *any* Applesoft expression with a non-negative value. For example, SQR(3*X+5) is perfectly acceptable provided that the expression 3*X+5 produces a non-negative value.

Note that the argument of a function must be enclosed in parentheses. In its evaluation of a mathematical function, the APPLE first evaluates the argument and then the function, using the value previously obtained for the argument. Some functions have a limitation on the value of the argument. Such limitations will be indicated as the functions are introduced.

Order of Operations

What is the value of 2+20/4? Should the 2 be added first to the 20 and then the division performed afterward, or should the 20 first be divided by 4 and then be increased by 2? The latter procedure is correct because division is carried out before addition. When parentheses are used, the operations in the innermost parentheses are completed first. For example, (2+20)/4 = 22/4 = 5.5.

The APPLE performs arithmetic operations in the same order as that employed by mathematicians. Quantities in parentheses are evaluated first (starting from the innermost), followed by raising to a power, then by multiplication and division, and finally by addition and subtraction. Operations of equal priority are carried out from left to right. For example:

6/3*2	The result is 4. Although the answer might seem to be 6/6=1, the computer starts at the left and performs the division first, then the result of the division is multiplied by 2.
3 * (5 + 6)	The result is 33. The computer first adds 5 and 6 and then multiplies the sum by 3.
5 + (3*(6/2))	The result is 14. The computer first divides 6 by 2, the numbers within the innermost parentheses. Next it multiplies that result by 3 and finally adds 5.
12 + 4/0	The result is an error message. The computer does not divide by zero.
2↑3↑2	The result is 64 just as it would be for (2↑3)↑2. Again, the left-to-right rule is in operation.

SGN and ABS

In some situations it may be necessary to know if a variable is positive or negative. The SGN function has only three possible values: 1, 0, and −1.

SGN(X) = 1	if $X>0$
SGN(X) = 0	if $X=0$
SGN(X) = -1	if $X<0$

PROGRAM 5.2

This program finds the SGN of the numbers from 20 to −20, incrementing by −5.

```
10  FOR X = 20 TO  - 20 STEP  - 5
20 A =  SGN (X)
30  PRINT A;" ";
40  NEXT X

]RUN
1 1 1 1 0 -1 -1 -1 -1
]
```

The ABS function can be used to find the absolute value of a number. The ABS function yields values according to the rule:

ABS(X) = X	if X>=0
ABS(X) = −1*X	if X<0

PROGRAM 5.3

This program illustrates the use of the ABS function.

```
10  FOR X =  - 20 TO 20 STEP 5
20 A =  ABS (X)
30  PRINT A;" ";
40  NEXT X

]RUN
20 15 10 5 0 5 10 15 20
```

Trigonometric Functions: SIN, COS, TAN

The APPLE is able to find the values of several trigonometric functions. Typing SIN(X), COS(X) or TAN(X) will produce the value of the sine, cosine, or tangent of the angle X, where X is measured in radians. To convert an angle from degrees to radians, multiply it by 3.14159265 . . . and then divide the result by 180 (180 degrees equals π radians).

PROGRAM 5.4

The following program illustrates these functions.

```
10  INPUT "VALUE? ";A
20 X = A * 3.1415926 / 180
30  PRINT A;" DEGREES= ";X;" RADIANS"
40  PRINT "SIN(";A;")="; SIN (X)
50  PRINT "COS(";A;")="; COS (X)
60  PRINT "TAN(";A;")="; TAN (X)
70  PRINT
80  GOTO 10

]RUN
VALUE? 30
30 DEGREES= .523598767 RADIANS
SIN(30)=.499999992
COS(30)=.866025408
TAN(30)=.577350257

VALUE? 45
45 DEGREES= .78539815 RADIANS
SIN(45)=.707106772
COS(45)=.707106791
TAN(45)=.999999972

VALUE?

BREAK IN 10
```

Notice the rounding error that occurs in the output.

ATN

The only inverse trigonometric function supplied with APPLESOFT is the principal arctangent function ATN. To find the angle whose tangent is (X), type ATN(X). The value produced by the ATN function is in radians. Thus, the arctangent of 1 is $\pi/4$ radians = .785398163. To convert an angle from radians to degrees, multiply it by 180 and then divide the result by 3.14159265. The ATN function, just like the principal arctangent function in mathematics, gives values only between $-\pi/2$ and $\pi/2$ radians. There is no limitation on the value that the argument may assume.

PROGRAM 5.5

This program finds the angle whose tangent is entered and prints the result in degrees.

```
10  INPUT T
20 X =  ATN (T)
30 A = X * 180 / 3.14159265
40  PRINT "THE ANGLE WHOSE TANGENT IS ";T;" IS ";A;" DEGREES."
50  GOTO 10

]RUN
?1
THE ANGLE WHOSE TANGENT IS 1 IS 45.0000001 DEGREES.
?0
THE ANGLE WHOSE TANGENT IS 0 IS 0 DEGREES.
?3
THE ANGLE WHOSE TANGENT IS 3 IS 71.5650513 DEGREES.
?

BREAK IN 10
```

To find the principal arcsine of a number on the APPLE one must use the following identity from trigonometry:

$$\text{arcsine}(X) = \arctan \frac{X}{\sqrt{1 - X^2}}$$

Therefore, in order to find the principal angle whose sine is X, the expression ATN(X/SQR(1−X↑2)) is used. This angle will be measured in radians and will be between $-\pi/2$ and $\pi/2$. The value of X, however, must be between −1 and 1, not inclusive.

To find the arccosine of X, use the expression ATN(SQR(1−X↑2)/X). This gives the angle which is between $-\pi/2$ and $\pi/2$ (whose cosine is X). In this expression, X must be between −1 and 1, inclusive, but not equal to 0.

PROGRAM 5.6

This program finds the arcsine and arccosine of X in both radians and degrees.

```
10  INPUT X
20 S =  ATN (X /  SQR (1 - X ^ 2))
30 C =  ATN ( SQR (1 - X ^ 2) / X)
40  PRINT "THE ANGLE WHOSE SINE IS ";X;" IS ";S;" RADIANS"
50  PRINT "THE ANGLE WHOSE COSINE IS ";X;" IS ";C;" RADIANS"
60  PRINT "THE ANGLE WHOSE SINE IS ";X;" IS ";S * 180 / 3.141592
65;" DEGREES"
70  PRINT "THE ANGLE WHOSE COSINE IS ";X;" IS ";C * 180 / 3.1415
9265;" DEGREES"
80  GOTO 10

]RUN
?0.5
THE ANGLE WHOSE SINE IS .5 IS .523598776 RADIANS
THE ANGLE WHOSE COSINE IS .5 IS 1.04719755 RADIANS
THE ANGLE WHOSE SINE IS .5 IS 30 DEGREES
THE ANGLE WHOSE COSINE IS .5 IS 60.0000001 DEGREES
?0.8
THE ANGLE WHOSE SINE IS .8 IS .927295218 RADIANS
THE ANGLE WHOSE COSINE IS .8 IS .643501109 RADIANS
THE ANGLE WHOSE SINE IS .8 IS 53.1301025 DEGREES
THE ANGLE WHOSE COSINE IS .8 IS 36.8698977 DEGREES
?

BREAK IN 10
```

Logarithms and the Exponential Function: LOG, EXP

The function LOG can be used to find natural logarithms, that is, logarithms to the base e. To find the natural logarithm of X, type LOG(X). Do not confuse the natural logarithm with the common logarithm usually studied in a second year algebra course. The common logarithm, that is, logarithm to base 10, can be found from the natural logarithm by using the formula:

$$\log_{10}(X) = \frac{\ln(X)}{\ln(10)}$$

where ln(x) designates the natural logarithm of X. Therefore, to find $\log_{10}$ (X) simply type LOG(X)/LOG(10). The argument in the LOG function must always be positive.

The function, EXP, can be used to find values of the exponential function, e^x,where e = 2.71828. This number is the same as the base of the natural logarithm function. To find e^x, type EXP(X).

PROGRAM 5.7

This program illustrates the use of the above functions.

```
10  INPUT X
20  PRINT "LN(X)="; LOG (X)
30  PRINT "E^X="; EXP (X)
40  GOTO 10

]RUN
?1
LN(X)=0
E^X=2.71828183
?0.5
LN(X)=-.69314718
E^X=1.64872127
?

BREAK IN 10
```

PROGRAM 5.8

This program illustrates how a common logarithm can be found.

```
10  INPUT N
20 T =  LOG (N) /  LOG (10)
30  PRINT "THE COMMON LOG OF ";N;" IS ";T
40  GOTO 10

]RUN
?1000
THE COMMON LOG OF 1000 IS 3
?0.01
THE COMMON LOG OF .01 IS -2
?5
THE COMMON LOG OF 5 IS .698970004
?

BREAK IN 10
```

DEF

Several standard functions, such as SQR, ABS, and LOG, have already been introduced in this chapter. In addition, the programmer can define other functions by using a DEF statement. The major advantage of DEF lies in the fact that the expression for the function need only be written once, even though the function can be evaluated at more than one location within the program. The form of a DEF statement is:

DEF FN <function name> (variable name) = <expression>

The function name may be any acceptable numeric variable name (e.g., FNA, FNF, FNG3). The variable name (i.e., the argument) following the function name must always appear within parentheses and may be any appropriate numeric variable.

In the following example,

10 DEF FNP(X)=X↑2 − 2*X − 1

P is the function name, X is the variable name, and X^2-2X-1 is the expression used to compute the function's value. For instance, when X = 5, FNP(X) = 14 because 5↑2 − 2*5 − 1 = 14.

PROGRAM 5.9

The following program evaluates the polynomial function FNP(X) several times.

```
10  DEF  FN P(X) = X ^ 2 - 2 * X - 1
20  PRINT "X","FNP(X)"
30  FOR A = 1 TO 5
40  PRINT A, FN P(A)
50  NEXT A
60  INPUT X
70  PRINT  FN P(X)

]RUN
X               FNP(X)
1               -2
2               -1
3               2
4               7
5               14
?-10
119
```

When the function is evaluated on line 40, the variable in parentheses is called A. When it is evaluated on line 70, the variable is called X. The name of the variable in parentheses may be the same as or different from the variable name used in the DEF statement. Note also that if the DEF statement were not used, the formula on line 10 would have to appear twice (lines 40 and 70). Economy results from the fact that the function is evaluated on more than one line.

Another advantage obtained by the use of the DEF statement is that it can be retyped easily to define a different function. This is illustrated by re-running Program 5.9 with line 10 changed to:

```
]10 DEF FNP(X)=X^3-5*X^2+1

]RUN
X                   FNP(X)
1                   -3
2                   -11
3                   -17
4                   -15
5                   1
?

BREAK IN 60
]
```

EXERCISES

PART A

1. Have the computer generate the following output. Be sure to prevent a negative input.

```
]RUN
?4
N = 4              SQUARE ROOTS = + OR - 2
```

2. Write a program which prints the integers from 121 to 144, inclusive, and their respective square roots. Label each column of the output.

3. Perform each of the following computations on paper. Check your results by using immediate mode on the computer.

   (A) 3↑2↑3
   (B) 5 - 4↑2
   (C) 3*(5 + 16)
   (D) 5 + 3 * 6/2
   (E) 640/10/2 * 5
   (F) 5 + 3 * 4 - 1
   (G) 2↑3↑2
   (H) 2↑(3↑2)
   (I) 64/4 * 0.5 + ((1 + 5) * 2↑3) * 1/(2 * 4)

4. Input a number N. If N is zero, print 0. Otherwise, print ABS(N)/N. What does the program do?

5. Input a number N, and print the product of SGN(N) and N. What does this program do?

6. Input a number N, square it, and print the square root of the result. What should the program produce?

7. Print a table consisting of 2 columns with headings showing each angle in radians and degrees. The angles in radians are to be 0, .25, .5, .75, . . ., 3.0. Remember that 180° = 3.14159 radians.

8. Input an angle in degrees and convert it to a fraction of a revolution (1 rev. = 360°) and to radians.

9. Input an angle in degrees. Of the three functions sine, cosine, and tangent, print the value of the one which has the greatest value.

10. For angles from 0° to 180°, at intervals of 10°, print the angle in degrees, the sine, the cosine, and the sum of their squares in columns with headings. What patterns emerge?

11. Input two numbers (A, B). Print the quantity F(B)-F(A), given that $F(X) = 9X^3 - 7X^2 + 4X - 1$.

12. Input a number N. Print the values of F(N) and F(F(N)), where F(X) = 20 * SQR (ABS(X))—10 * SGN (X) + 5 * INT (X).

13. Print a table (with headings) of X, the natural logarithm of X, and the exponential function of X for X = 1 to 15.

14. Print a table (with headings) of X, the logarithm of X to the base 10, and 10 raised to the power X for X = 1 to 15.

PART B

15. What is the exact output for the following program? Check by running the program.

```
10  READ A,B,C,D
20  PRINT  SQR (A), INT (B), SQR ( INT (C)), INT ( SQR (D))
30  DATA  25,-3.4,9.7,24
```

16. Print the square roots of the integers from 50 to 60, inclusive.

17. What is the exact output for the following program? Check by running the program.

```
10  DEF  FN F(N) = 3 * N - 6
20  FOR X =  - 4 TO 6 STEP 2
30  IF  FN F(X) > 0 THEN  PRINT "FNF(";X;") IS POSITIVE"
40  IF  FN F(X) = 0 THEN  PRINT "FNF(";X;") IS ZERO"
50  IF  FN F(X) < 0 THEN  PRINT "FNF(";X;") IS NEGATIVE"
60  NEXT X
```

18. Input a number, and print the square root, sign, log, and sine of the number. For example:

```
]RUN
?16
SQR(16) = 4
SGN(16) = 1
LOG(16) = 2.77258872
SIN(16) = -.287903315
```

19. What is the exact output for the following program? Check by running the program.

```
10  FOR X =  - 3 TO 4
20  READ A
25  PRINT  SGN (X) *  ABS (X),
30  NEXT X
40  DATA  3,-5,1,6,-2,4,-9,5
```

20. Using three user-defined functions, have the computer evaluate the following for the integers from -10 to 10.

$$X^2 + 3X + 2$$

$$LOG(X^2+1) - X$$

$$ATN(SIN(X))$$

21. The following program is designed to print a table of square roots for all the integers between 1 and 100, inclusive. However, there are some errors. The output should resemble the following:

```
]RUN
NUMBER                SQUARE ROOT
1                     1
2                     1.41421356
.                     .
.                     .
100                   10

— — — — — — — — — — — — — — — —

20   FOR X = 1 TO 100
30   PRINT NUMBER,SQUAREROOT
40   PRINT X; SQR (X)
50   NEXT
```

22. Write a program to convert from polar to rectangular coordinates (i.e., from (r,Θ) to (X,Y)).

23. If two functions, f and g, are inverse to each other, the following relations hold: $f(g(x)) = x$ and $g(f(x)) = x$.

(a) Tabulate the values of the following quantities for X = -5 to 10: X, EXP(X), LOG(EXP(X)).
(b) Print a table for X = 1 to 151 of X, LOG(X), EXP(LOG(X)), using STEP 10.
(c) Do EXP and LOG appear to be inverse to each other?
(d) Could X be zero or negative in (b)?

24. Produce your own sequence of random numbers without using the RND command. To do this let X vary from 1 to 100 in steps of 1. Obtain SIN(X) and multiply this by 1000, calling the absolute value of the product Y. Divide INT(Y) by 16, and let the remainder R serve as your random number. Hint: the remainder of A ÷ B is A/B—INT (A/B).

25. Six year old Dennis the Menace has decided to invest 50¢ in the Last Chew bubble gum company. Starting with the 11th year, he withdraws 5¢ at the beginning of each year. His money earns 8% interest compounded continually. The formula for interest compounded continually is $P = P_0e^{it}$, where t is the elapsed time in years, P_0 is the initial deposit, P is the amount at time t, and i is the interest rate. In this case the formula would be $P=P_0e^{.08t}$. How much is Dennis's deposit worth after 50 years?

26. Use the SIN function to generate the following:

```
]RUN
                     SHAZAM!
                        SHAZAM!
                            SHAZAM!
                                SHAZAM!
                                   SHAZAM!
                                     SHAZAM!
                                       SHAZAM!
                                        SHAZAM!
                                        SHAZAM!
                                        SHAZAM!
                                       SHAZAM!
                                     SHAZAM!
                                  SHAZAM!
                               SHAZAM!
                           SHAZAM!
                       SHAZAM!
                   SHAZAM!
               SHAZAM!
            SHAZAM!
        SHAZAM!
     SHAZAM!
   SHAZAM!
 SHAZAM!
 SHAZAM!
 SHAZAM!
 SHAZAM!
   SHAZAM!
     SHAZAM!
        SHAZAM!
           SHAZAM!
               SHAZAM!
                   SHAZAM!
```

27. Write a program to convert from rectangular to polar coordinates (i.e., from (X,Y) to (r, θ)).

28. Write a program which will solve a triangle (compute the unknown sides and angles) if two sides and the included angle are input. Modify the program to solve for the unknown sides and angles for the following situations:
(a) input two angles and any side,
(b) input three sides.

29. Input X, and print the Arcsine, Arccosine, and Arctangent of X.

6 GRAPHICS

Graphs are useful for simplifying the presentation and analysis of large bodies of data. Relationships hidden in a mass of information are often uncovered when the information is presented in graphical form. This chapter introduces the statements needed for graphing and shows how graphing programs utilize them.

The APPLE provides two modes for displaying graphs: low and high resolution. The low resolution mode divides the graphing area into 40 rows, each row being further subdivided into 40 rectangular areas shaped like 'bricks.' Each brick represents a point and may be filled with any of 16 different colors. The high resolution mode divides the graphing area into very small dots which may be plotted in 8 different colors. Statements are available for plotting lines and points in both modes. Low resolution mode is usually used to produce bar graphs, while the high resolution mode is used to graph mathematical functions where greater detail and higher precision are desired.

If the APPLE is being used with a black and white video display, the colors referred to in this chapter will be displayed as various shades of gray and black. The description of the color variables is, therefore, still useful.

LOW RESOLUTION GRAPHICS

The low resolution mode partitions the screen into an invisible 40 by 40 grid and gives the user a selection of 16 colors which can be employed to fill a rectangle in the grid. The valid X and Y values of the grid range between 0 and 39, inclusive, where X is the horizontal coordinate and Y the vertical coordinate. The origin (0,0) of the grid is located in the upper-left corner of the display screen. The grid occupies the top portion of the screen, while the bottom 4 lines of the screen contain a small 'text window' for program lines and character output. All of the graphing statements discussed may be used either in immediate mode or in a program.

GR

In order to enter the low resolution mode, the GR statement is used either in immediate mode or in a program. GR will clear the 40 x 40 grid on the user's video display in preparation for plotting. For example,

```
20 GR
```

erases the video screen and prepares the computer to accept low resolution statements.

TEXT and HOME

In order to leave either of the two graphics modes and return to normal programming mode, the TEXT statement is used. The line

```
40 TEXT
```

resets the computer to normal mode but does not completely clear the screen. The graphs currently on the screen will be lost and the screen will be filled with miscellaneous characters and text. The HOME command can be used to clear the screen after the TEXT statement has been used.

COLOR

When plotting points and lines in low resolution mode, the COLOR variable can be used. A value between 0 and 15 is assigned to this variable to select one of 16 colors. The COLOR variable is set like any other variable. For example, the line

```
120 COLOR = 9
```

will set the value of the COLOR variable to 9. Thereafter, all points plotted will be orange until the value of COLOR is changed. The COLOR variable is set to zero automatically when the GR statement is used. The valid colors are:

0-Black	4-Dark Green	8-Brown	12-Green
1-Red	5-Grey	9-Orange	13-Yellow
2-Dark Blue	6-Medium Blue	10-Grey	14-Aqua
3-Purple	7-Light Blue	11-Pink	15-White

PLOT

In low resolution plotting, the PLOT statement is used to plot a single brick-shaped area on the display screen in the 40 x 40 grid. The color of the brick is determined by the value of the COLOR variable. The statement

```
20 PLOT X,Y
```

will plot a brick at the coordinates (X,Y). Remember that the values for X and Y range from 0 to 39.

PROGRAM 6.1

The following program will plot 3 red bricks on the display screen at the points (12,32), (29,11), and (1,2).

```
10  GR
20  COLOR= 1
30  PLOT 12,32
40  PLOT 29,11
50  PLOT 1,2
```

HLIN

The HLIN statement is used to plot a low resolution horizontal line of bricks. The statement

45 HLIN X1,X2 AT Y

will plot a horizontal line from point (X1,Y) to (X2,Y). The color of the line will be the last one set by the COLOR variable before the HLIN statement is executed. For example,

30 HLIN 10,30 AT 22

will draw a line from coordinates (10,22) to (30,22). If COLOR = 9 when line 30 is executed, then the line will be orange.

VLIN

The VLIN statement operates similarly to the HLIN statement but produces a vertical line. The statement

110 VLIN Y1,Y2 AT X

will plot a vertical line from point (X,Y1) to (X,Y2). The color of the line will depend upon the last setting of the COLOR variable. For example,

180 VLIN 0,39 AT 21

will draw a vertical line from coordinates (21,0) to (21,39). Assuming that COLOR = 1 when line 180 is executed, a red line will be produced.

SCRN

The SCRN function makes it possible for a program to determine the color of a particular block in the 40 x 40 grid. Given coordinates (X,Y), the SCRN function will return a value between 0 and 15 corresponding to the color value at the given point. The coordinates X and Y must be between 0 and 39, inclusive. The following statements illustrate various uses of the SCRN function.

```
10 C = SCRN(10,32)
80 PRINT "THE COLOR IS"; SCRN(18,Y2)
45 PRINT 16 * SCRN(18,2)—SCRN(I,J)
```

SCRN can be used in immediate mode by typing statements in the text window.

PROGRAM 6.2

This program demonstrates the various statements used in low resolution graphing.

```
10  GR
20  COLOR= 1
30  PLOT 20,12
40  HLIN 0,39 AT 30
50  COLOR= 15
60  HLIN 12,32 AT 32
70  VLIN 1,18 AT 24
80 C1 =  SCRN( 21,30)
90 C2 =  SCRN( 24,5)
100 C3 =  SCRN( 1,0)
110  PRINT "RED AT (21,30) = ";C1
120  PRINT "WHITE AT (24,5) = ";C2
130  PRINT "BLACK AT (1,0) = ";C3;
```

Line 10 prepares the display screen for graphing, while line 20 selects the color red. The plotting done by lines 30 and 40 will be in red. Line 30 graphs a point at (20,12), while line 40 draws a horizontal line from (0,30) to (39,30). Line 50 changes the color to white so that lines 60 and 70 will produce white lines, but what was plotted by lines 30 and 40 will remain red. Lines 80-120 examine and print the color of various points on the screen. Parts of the screen where nothing was plotted, including the point at (1,0), remain black.

REVIEW

1. Have the computer draw a green border around the edge of the graphing area. Make the border 1 'brick' wide.

2. Have the computer color the screen red except for a single blue point at coordinates (19,19).

3. Have the computer generate 15 vertical lines, one for each color except black.

HIGH RESOLUTION GRAPHICS

High resolution graphics enables the user to draw more finely detailed images than those drawn in low resolution graphics. This is true because the display screen is partitioned into a grid of dots which are smaller and far more numerous than the bricks used in low resolution graphics. There are two modes used in high resolution graphics. One mode utilizes the entire screen for a display grid of 192 rows by 280 columns. The other mode reserves a 4 line text window, which reduces the grid to 160 rows by 280 columns. As in low resolution graphics, the origin (0,0) is located in the upper-left corner of the screen.

HGR and HGR2

The HGR and HGR2 statements are used to switch the display screen into high resolution mode. The HGR statement reserves a text window at the bottom of the screen, while the HGR2 statement utilizes the entire screen for graphing. Both statements clear the high resolution graphing area. Valid examples are:

```
70 HGR2
and
45 HGR
```

At times it might be desirable to use the small text window supplied by the HGR statement, and then switch to HGR2 in order to use the entire screen for graphing. When the switch is made, what has already been plotted will be cleared from the screen. If the command POKE-16302,0 is used, however, the plotted points will be retained. The following line illustrates the use of the POKE statement:

```
140 POKE-16302,0
```

Refer to Appendix A for more information regarding POKE.

HCOLOR

When plotting in high resolution graphics, the HCOLOR variable is used for color selection. A range of 8 colors is available, numbered 0 through 7, inclusive. For example, the statement

```
139 HCOLOR = 1
```

will set the value of the HCOLOR variable to 1, thus selecting the color green. All subsequent plotting will be in green until the HCOLOR variable is changed. The valid colors for high resolution plotting are:

0-Black	2-Purple	4-Black	6-Blue
1-Green	3-White 1	5-Red	7-White 2

Because of variations in colors produced by different video displays, the colors produced may not agree exactly with those in the table.

HPLOT

The HPLOT statement is used for plotting both points and lines in high resolution graphics. The statement

```
20 HPLOT X,Y
```

will plot a single point at the coordinates (X,Y). The X-coordinate can vary from 0 to 279. If the 4 line text window is used, then the Y-coordinate can vary from 0 to 159; otherwise, Y can vary from 0 to 191. The HPLOT statement can be modified to draw lines. The statement

```
180 HPLOT X1,Y1 TO X2,Y2
```

draws a line from the point (X1,Y1) to (X2,Y2) with its color determined by the HCOLOR variable. Several connecting lines can be drawn in a single statement. For example, the statement

```
210 HPLOT X1,Y1 TO X2,Y2 TO X3,Y3
```

draws one line from (X1,Y1) to (X2,Y2) and another line from (X2,Y2) to (X3,Y3). The modifier TO can be added to the HPLOT statement as many times as neded (except for the restriction that a program line is limited to 239 characters).

If the first set of coordinates after the word HPLOT is omitted, a line is drawn from the last point plotted by a previous HPLOT statement to the point specified after the word TO. The color of the new line will be that of the last point plotted, and not the color corresponding to the most recent value of the HCOLOR variable. An example of this form of the HPLOT statement is:

```
40 HPLOT TO X,Y
```

Because of the limitations found in most video displays, there may be some difficulty with the color of points and vertical lines in high resolution. The difficulty may be avoided by plotting even numbered colors at points with even numbered X-coordinates, and odd numbered colors at points with odd numbered X-coordinates. For example, a red (COLOR = 5) line can be plotted successfully with an X-coordinate of 21 using the statement,

```
20 HPLOT 21,3 TO 21,12
```

Should we attempt to plot a red line with an X-coordinate of 22, the statement

```
20 HPLOT 22,3 TO 22,12
```

will plot a black line which cannot be seen against the screen's black background.

PROGRAM 6.3

The following program constructs a green border around the display area and plots a single blue point, using high resolution graphing statements.

```
10  HGR
20  HCOLOR= 1
30  HPLOT 1,1 TO 279,1 TO 279,159
40  HPLOT  TO 1,159
50  HPLOT  TO 1,1
60  HCOLOR= 6
70  HPLOT 140,80
```

Lines 30 through 50 draw the green border around the edge of the display screen. Note that the last point plotted before line 40 was (279,159) at line 30. Therefore, line 40 has the same effect as the statement,

40 HPLOT 279,159 TO 1,159

A similar comment applies at line 50. Line 70 plots a single blue point in the center of the display. Note that if line 30 is changed to

30 HPLOT 1,1 TO 278,1 TO 278,159

the right vertical side of the border might be black and thus not visible since an attempt has been made to plot an odd numbered color with an even numbered X-coordinate.

PROGRAM 6.4

The following program plots the function Y = 2X + 1. The axes are conventional, the positive X-axis pointing to the right and the positive Y-axis pointing upward.

```
10  HGR2 : HCOLOR= 5
20 XO = 135:YO = 100
30  REM  DRAW AXES
40  HPLOT O,YO TO 279,YO
50  HPLOT XO,O TO XO,191
60  REM  GRAPH FUNCTION
70  FOR X1 = O TO 279
80 X = X1 - XO
90 Y = 2 * X + 1
100 Y1 = YO - Y
110  IF (Y1 >  = O) AND (Y1 <  = 191) THEN  HPLOT X1,Y1
120  NEXT X1
```

Line 10 prepares the display screen for graphing and selects the color red. Line 20 places the origin (intersection of X and Y axes) at (X0,Y0). At this point on the screen, both X and Y are zero. The actual plotting of the axes is done by line 40 and 50. A loop is established at line 70 where values for X1 are generated. X is calculated by subtracting X0 from X1 so that Y can be calculated on line 90. At line 100, Y1 is calculated in preparation for plotting the point. Line 110 determines whether the values of X1 and Y1 fit into graphing area. If so, the point (X1,Y1) is plotted.

REVIEW

4. Allow the user to input two values, X and Y. Have the computer then take these two values and plot a point at the given coordinates (X,Y) with a randomly selected color.

5. Have the computer generate 7 horizontal lines, one for each possible color of high resolution graphics (except HCOLOR = 0). Each color should be separated by a black area 10 lines wide.

6. Modify Program 6.4 so that it will plot the equation $Y = (1/5)X^2 - 8$.

SHIFTING AND SCALING A GRAPH

A hand-drawn graph usually includes an X-axis drawn horizontally, a Y-axis drawn vertically, and a continuous curve drawn through a number of plotted points. There are some obvious limitations to graphs produced by the computer, (for example, the lack of connection between plotted points). The graphing area on the display screen contains a limited number of points available for plotting. Thus, certain adjustments of the X and Y-axes may be necessary to accommodate functions which produce values that exceed the number of graphing points available. This problem is solved by determining the domain (smallest and largest X values) and the range (smallest and largest Y values) for a function where Y = f(X) and then scaling the axes accordingly. These processes are referred to as shifting and scaling.

Shifting is achieved by subtracting the minimum value of Y from each Y value. For example, if a function has values between -10 and +15, Y minus the minimum value (Y-(-10)) shifts the graph to points between 0 and 25 on the Y-axis. This does not affect the shape of the graph.

Scaling, on the other hand, takes the difference between the largest and smallest values and divides this difference by one less than the number of points available for a particular axis. The one extra space allows the axis to start with the smallest plotted value. For example, if the interval between the largest and smallest Y values for a particular graph is 400 units and the display screen has only 192 vertical points for plotting, the 400 is divided by (192-1) or 191 to produce the proper scale. Approximately every 2 points on the graph's Y-axis corresponds to 1 point on the screen.

PROGRAM 6.5

The following program illustrates how the function Y = 150*SIN(X) is shifted and scaled to fit on the full high resolution screen.

```
10  HGR2 : HCOLOR= 3:PI = 3.14159
20  FOR X =  - 3 * PI TO 3 * PI STEP .05
30 Y = 150 *  SIN (X): REM   THE FUNCTION
40 YO = Y / (300 / 191): REM   SCALE Y-AXIS
50 YO = YO + 96: REM   SHIFT Y-AXIS
60 XO = X / (6 * PI / 279): REM   SCALE X-AXIS
70 XO = XO + 140: REM   SHIFT X-AXIS
80  HPLOT XO,YO
90  NEXT X

]RUN
```

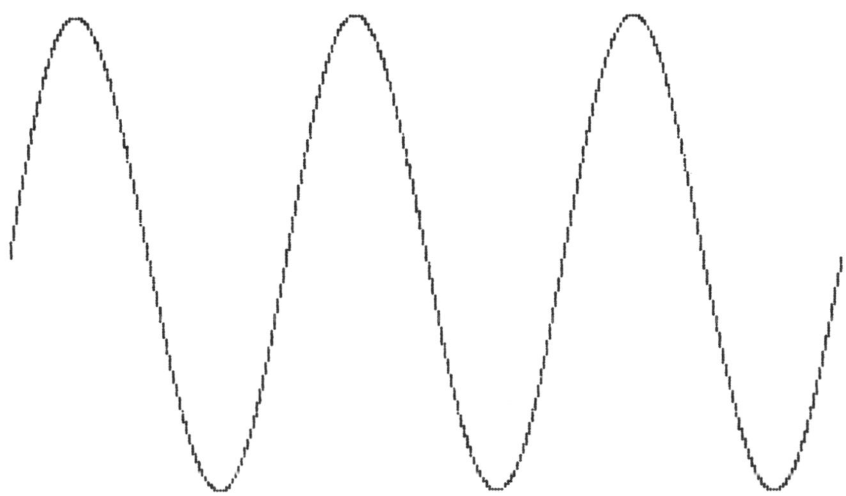

The function is evaluated at line 30 with a domain of -3π to 3π in increments of 0.05. The result (Y) is scaled by dividing Y by the ratio 300/191. The 300 represents the absolute range of the function. The 191 represents the vertical width of the screen minus 1. X is scaled in a similar fashion by line 60. Both X and Y are shifted by lines 70 and 50 respectively.

PROGRAM 6.6

This program plots the function Y = 1/X on the display screen. Note how the graph has been shifted and scaled.

```
10   HGR2 : HCOLOR= 3
20   HPLOT 140,0 TO 140,191
30   HPLOT 0,96 TO 279,96
40   FOR X =  - 12 TO 12 STEP .1
50   IF X = 0 THEN 140
60 Y = 1 / X: REM   FUNCTION
70 X1 = X / (24 / 279): REM   SCALE X-AXIS
80 X1 = X1 + 140: REM   SHIFT X-AXIS
90 Y1 = Y / (2 / 191): REM   SCALE Y-AXIS
100 Y1 = 96 - Y1: REM   SHIFT Y-AXIS
110  IF X1 < 0 OR X1 > 279 THEN 140
120  IF Y1 < 0 OR Y1 > 191 THEN 140
130  HPLOT X1,Y1
140  NEXT X

]RUN
```

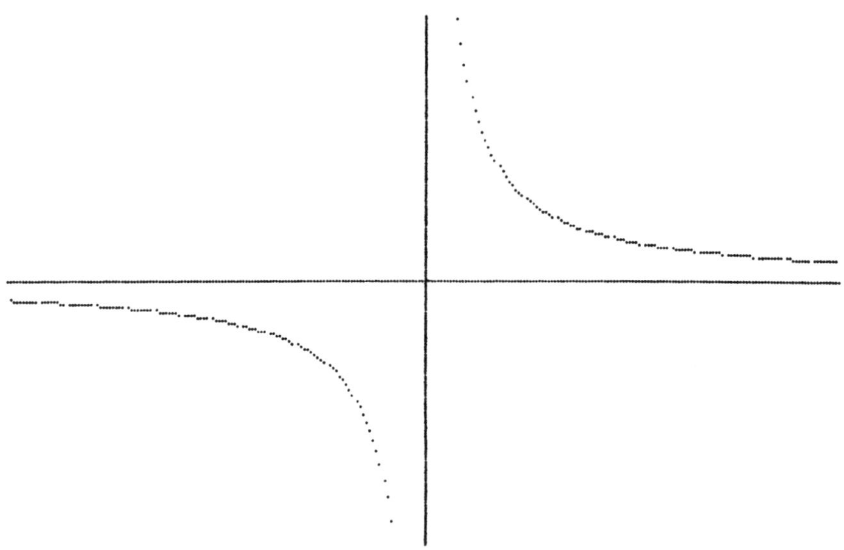

The analysis of this program is left as an exercise for the reader.

EXERCISES

PART A

1. Have the computer draw a solid orange rectangle with its upper left corner at (19,10), a length of 3 columns, and a height of 2 rows.

2. Have the computer draw a green letter L about two inches high in the upper left corner of the screen.

3. Have the computer draw a small letter i about an inch high with the dot at (15,18).

4. Using high resolution mode draw a blue vertical line and a white horizontal line which intersect at (140,80).

5. Have the computer construct a blue right triangle with the altitude from (250,20) to (250,110) and the base from (250,110) to (130,110). Use only one HPLOT statement.

6. In high resolution mode draw a violet letter A with the top at (40,40) and the lowest point of the left side at (10,130).

7. Using high resolution graphics have the computer produce the following figure:

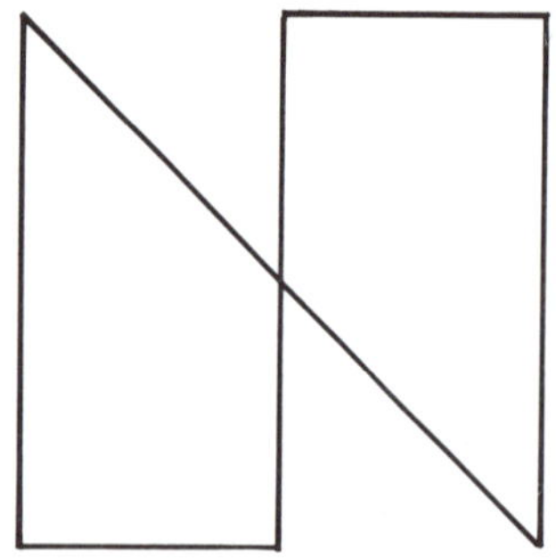

8. Have the computer generate 200 random integers between 1 and 10, inclusive. Using low resolution graphics, plot a properly labeled bar graph showing the number of occurrences of each random number.

9. Using program 6.4 as a guide, plot the graph of $Y = 2^X$

PART B

10. At times, it might be necessary to leave a computer temporarily. To signify that it is being used, leave the message (IN USE) printed on the screen in large block letters at least two inches high.

11. The following table shows production output per day for each employee of Papa's Pizza Parlor. Plot a bar graph showing the average output per week for each of Papa's employees.

Employee	Pizza Production
Greer	18,12,9,10,16,22,14
McPherson	12,21,19,16,28,20,22
Rady	18,20,14,19,11,16,23
Wyncott	23,27,18,16,21,14,24

12. Allow the user to enter 3 numbers: A, B, and R. Have the computer plot a circle of radius R with its center at (A,B). (Hint: The equation of a circle with center (A,B) and radius R is $(X-A)^2 + (Y-B)^2 = R^2$.)

13. Using low resolution graphics have the computer generate an 18 x 18 rectangular dart board using the colors 1 through 5, where grey (COLOR 5) occupies the center of the board. Each color from 4 to 1 should form a rectangular border around the colors inside it. Have the computer take 10 random shots at points on the board. Using the SCRN function, total the computer's score (i.e., if the point of impact is within the grey

area, the computer scores 5 points; if within the dark green area, the computer scores 4 points, etc.). Show where each dart hits by plotting a black brick at the point of impact.

14. Print a graph of Y = SIN(n πX), where n is chosen by the user from the set (-1,1,1/2,1/4). The units of length for the X and Y axes need not be the same. The periodic nature of the sine function should be indicated on your graph.

15. Produce the following graphs with numbered X and Y axes and the origin properly centered. (Hint: see Program 6.4).

    (A) Print a graph of Y = SGN(X)
    (B) Print a graph of Y = ATN(X)
    (C) Print a graph of Y = INT(X)

16. Have the computer fill the first 19 columns of the low resolution screen with randomly colored bricks.

    (A) Using the SCRN function, duplicate the left portion of the screen on the right side of the screen in columns 21 through 39.
    (B) Rewrite part A such that the right portion of the screen is a mirror image of the left portion.

17. The ancient puzzle 'Towers of Hanoi' uses 5 different sized disks and 3 pegs. The 5 disks are initially stacked on the left peg in order of decreasing size. The object of the

game is to move all of the disks to the right peg. Only 1 disk can be moved at a time and a larger disk cannot be placed on top of a smaller disk.

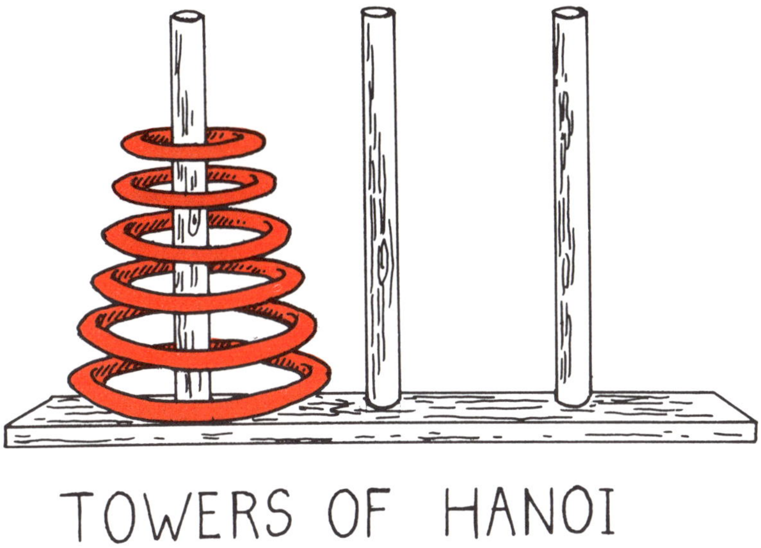

Initial Configuration for Towers of Hanoi

(A) Write a program using low resolution graphics that will draw a green base with green pegs and plot the initial configuration of 5 red disks on the left tower.

(B) Expand the program from part A to allow movement of the disks. The user should be able to enter two values (P and Q). This should cause the top disk on tower P to be moved to the top of the stack on tower Q. (Hint: Set up a subscripted variable A(X,Y) with maximum values X=3, Y=5). There are 15 possible slots for disks; 3 towers, 5 slots per tower. When a slot is occupied, the subscripted variable A(X,Y) should contain the disk number occupying that slot (1-5). If the slot is free, the appropriate position in A(X,Y) should contain a zero).

7 SUBROUTINES AND FLOWCHARTING

Writing long, complex programs may require special programming techniques. It is often helpful to divide these programs into sections, called subroutines. Subroutines are useful because they perform a specified task in a limited number of lines and may be accessed from anywhere in the program. A long program may be divided into a main section and a series of subroutines. The main section directs the order in which the subroutines do their specialized jobs. This type of organization usually reduces the size of a program because the lines needed to perform a certain task have only to be placed once in a subroutine, even though the task may be performed several times.

Before composing complicated or lengthy programs, it is frequently helpful to draw a diagram that outlines the logic to be used in constructing the program. Such diagrams, called flow charts, are especially helpful when a program contains subroutines.

GOSUB-RETURN

In the case of programs whose various portions are repeated at different places, it may be efficient to use a subroutine. A subroutine is entered by the command GOSUB <line number> and exited on the command RETURN. For example:

```
10 ........
20  GOSUB 200
30 ........
40 ........
200 .......
210 .......
220 .......
230  RETURN
999  END
```

The skeleton program given above illustrates the use of a subroutine. At line 20 the program jumps to the subroutine which begins on line 200, executes the subroutine, and then returns on line 230 to the body of the program at line 30. It is legal to use more than one RETURN statement within a subroutine. You should remember that the computer always returns to the first statement after the GOSUB statement which caused the subroutine to be executed. The only difference between GOSUB and the GOTO statement is that GOSUB permits the use of RETURN whereas GOTO does not. Subroutines are usually placed towards the bottom of a program. They may be written so that one subroutine can access another.

PROGRAM 7.1

Given the numbers of pennies, nickels, dimes, and quarters as input, this program will output the total amount of money represented by these coins. One subroutine processes and reports the amount of money involved for each of the four types of coins.

```
10 A$ = "PENNIES":V = 1
20   GOSUB 200
30 A$ = "NICKELS":V = 5
40   GOSUB 200
50 A$ = "DIMES":V = 10
60   GOSUB 200
70 A$ = "QUARTERS":V = 25
80   GOSUB 200
90   PRINT "THE TOTAL VALUE WAS $";T / 100
100   END
200   INPUT "NUMBER OF COINS? ";N
210   PRINT N;" ";A$;" = ";N * V;" CENTS"
220 T = T + N * V
230   RETURN

]RUN
NUMBER OF COINS? 4
4 PENNIES = 4 CENTS
NUMBER OF COINS? 7
7 NICKELS = 35 CENTS
NUMBER OF COINS? 2
2 DIMES = 20 CENTS
NUMBER OF COINS? 3
3 QUARTERS = 75 CENTS
THE TOTAL VALUE WAS $1.34
```

Line 10 assigns the type (A$) and value (V) of the first coin. Line 20 causes a jump to the subroutine, which begins at line 200 where the number of coins is input. Line 210 prints information about the particular coin being considered, and line 220 adds its contribution to the previous total value of all coins up to this point. Line 230 returns the program back to the line following the most recently used GOSUB statement. This entire process, beginning at line 200, repeats itself three more times, and then the dollar total is printed. What would happen if line 100 were deleted?

ON—GOTO

The GOTO statement allows a program to jump to a single specified line. The ON—GOTO statement allows jumps to one of several lines, depending on the value of a variable at the time the statement is encountered. This statement takes the form:

ON <variable> GOTO <list of line numbers>

For example:

```
50 ON X GOTO 100, 120, 140,160
```

If X = 1, the program jumps to line 100; if X = 2, it jumps to line 120, and so on. Note that X should not be less than one or greater than four.

PROGRAM 7.2

This program simulates the random path taken by a mouse through the following maze:

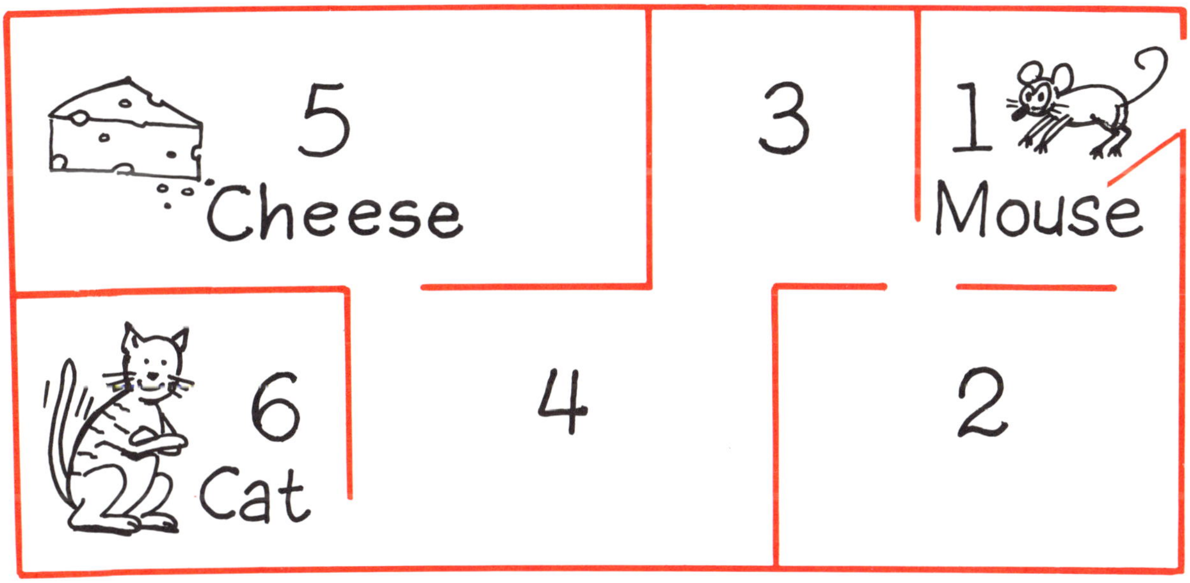

Once the mouse enters the maze, the door is shut. The mouse wanders until it either finds the cheese or stumbles upon the cat.

```
100  PRINT 1,
110 X =  INT ( RND (1) * 2 + 1)
120  ON X GOTO 200,300
200  PRINT 2,
210 X =  INT ( RND (1) * 2 + 1)
220  ON X GOTO 100,300
300  PRINT 3,
310 X =  INT ( RND (1) * 3 + 1)
320  ON X GOTO 100,200,400
400  PRINT 4,
410 X =  INT ( RND (1) * 3 + 1)
420  ON X GOTO 300,500,600
500  PRINT 5
510  PRINT "THE MOUSE IS GORGING ITSELF!"
520  END
600  PRINT 6
610  PRINT "THE CAT HAS BEEN WOKEN UP BY ITS LUNCH."

]RUN
1               3               2               3               2
 3               4               3               2
3               1               3               2               1
 2               1               3               4
6
THE CAT HAS BEEN WOKEN UP BY ITS LUNCH.
```

At line 100, the program prints a 1 to indicate that the mouse is in room #1. Line 110 randomly picks either the number 1 or the number 2. The ON GOTO statement at line 120 sends program execution to line 200 if X=1 and to 300 if X=2; lines 200 and 300 correspond to rooms 2 and 3, respectively. Once in one of the other rooms, the program prints the room number and decides where the mouse will go from there. Execution continues until the mouse finds itself either in room #5 or room #6.

ON—GOSUB

The ON—GOSUB statement operates in much the same way as the ON—GOTO statement. If there are a number of subroutines in a program, they can be entered using the ON—GOSUB statement.

```
50 ON X GOSUB 300, 400, 500
```

If X = 1, the program jumps to the first subroutine at line 300; if X = 2, to the second subroutine at line 400; and if X = 3, to the third subroutine at line 500. When the subroutine is completed, the RETURN statement directs the program back to the first statement after line 50.

FLOWCHARTING

As programs become more complex, it becomes especially easy to forget important details or to lose track of the direction that the program must take. Such problems can be avoided by preparing an outline in the form of a flow chart before the program is actually written.

Symbols for Flowcharting

A large program often consists of two parts; the main body of the program in one, and its functions and subroutines in the other. Usually the main body comes first and the functions and subroutines second. Execution of the main body should flow from top to bottom. Any GOTO statements should send execution to a point before the GOTO, and not after it. This format makes a program easier to be read and, in many cases, more efficient. To write such a program the programmer must first have a comprehensible outline. One way to construct an outline is to draw what is called a flow chart. A flow chart consists of various symbols and words which graphically show what the program is to do. Because of their pictorial form, flow charts make potential deficiencies in a program easy to spot.

There are five different symbols in flowcharting. The first symbol is 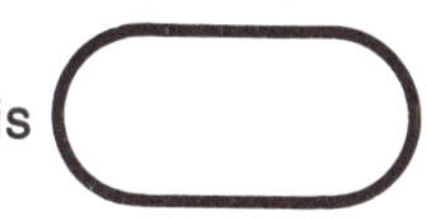. This is a terminator which indicates the beginning or end of a program or subroutine. The second symbol is  and is called the Input/Output or I/O symbol. This indicates that data is either entering or leaving the program. Generally, it designates an operation with the disk or tape, or an INPUT, READ, or PRINT statement. The following is a flow chart to input a number (X) and print the number multiplied by three.

One possible program for this flow chart would be the following:

```
10 INPUT X
20 PRINT 3*X
```

Note the arrows in the flow chart which indicate the direction of flow in the program. Also note that the flow chart proceeds from left to right. In general, flow charts proceed from left to right or from top to bottom. In more complex examples, they may move both from left to right and from top to bottom.

The next symbol is the process symbol which indicates the processing of some data

. It is the most general of the five symbols and is used whenever one of the other four more specific symbols does not apply. The following is a flow chart for a program which allows the user to input a student's name and four course grades. It computes the average of the grades (process symbol), prints the student's name and average, and then returns to begin the cycle again. The accompanying program was written based upon the flow chart.

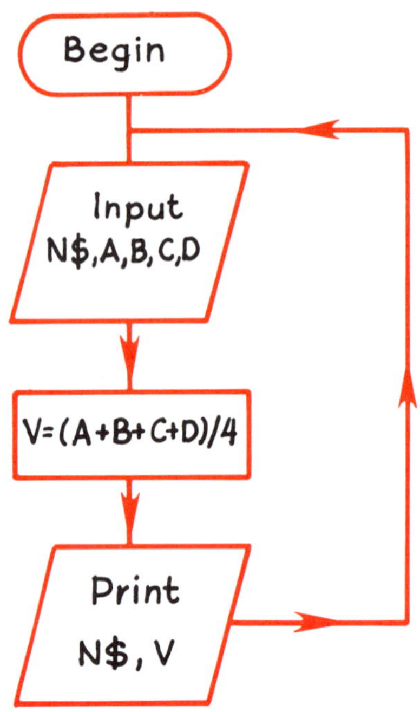


```
10  INPUT "NAME AND 4 GRADES: ";N$,A,B,C,D
20 V = (A + B + C + D) / 4
30  PRINT N$,V
40  GOTO 10
```

The fourth symbol, 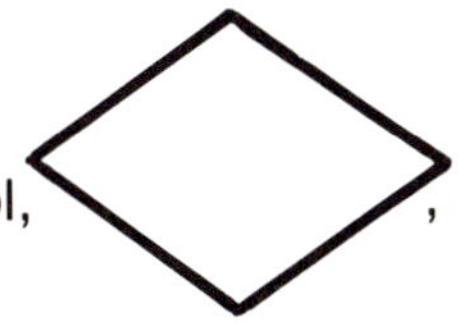, designates a conditional, indicating that a decision is to be made. The IF . . . THEN statement is one type of conditional. The following flow chart specifies a number that is input and then goes on to determine if it be negative or not.

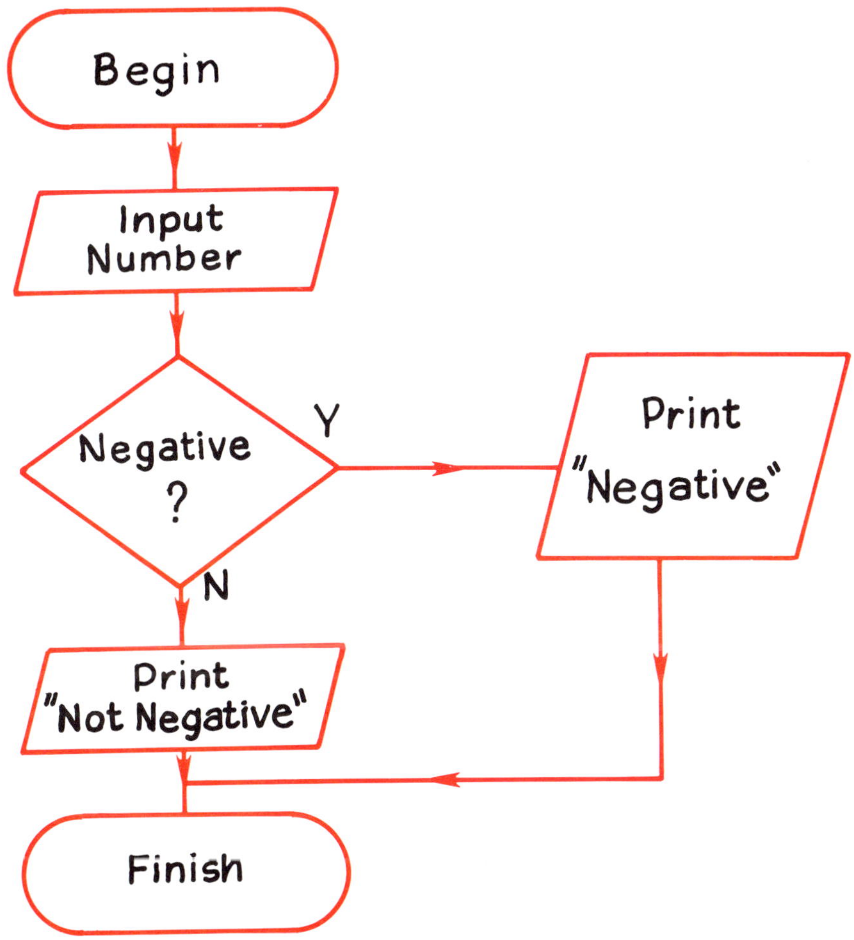


```
10  INPUT X
20  IF X < 0 THEN  PRINT "NEGATIVE": END
30  PRINT "NOT NEGATIVE"
```

The conditional symbol always has two or more arrows coming from it. In this case there are two such arrows, labeled Y for YES and N for NO.

The NEXT X portion of a FOR . . . TO, NEXT loop is also a conditional. The flow chart and accompanying program ask the user to input a number and then print four multiples of the number.

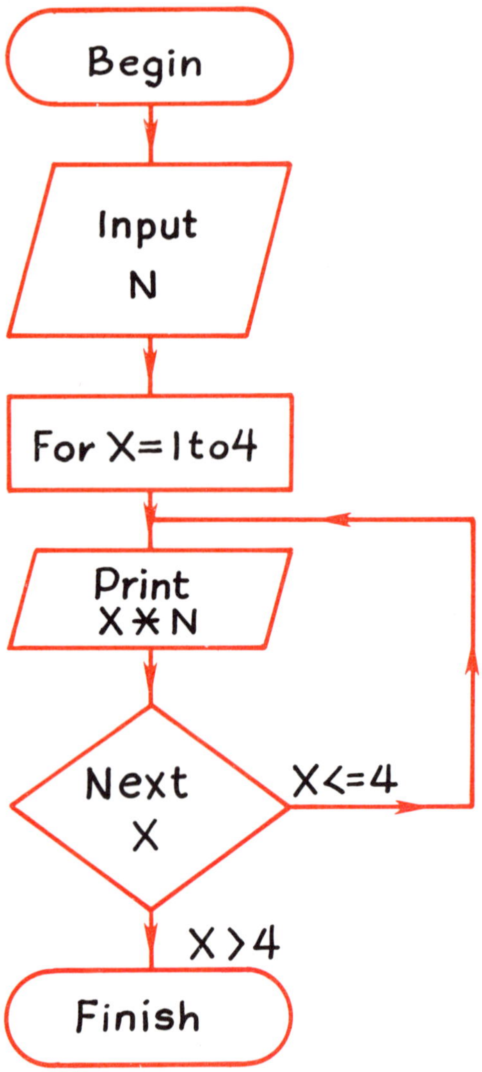


```
10   INPUT N
20   FOR X = 1 TO 4
30   PRINT X * N
40   NEXT X
```

Each time the conditional symbol is reached, X is incremented and a decision is made based on its new value. If X is 4 or less, the loop continues and another result is printed; if X exceeds 4, the run ends. The two exit symbols from the conditional allow these two possibilities.

The last symbol is the connector symbol, which is a circle:  . It is used to connect separate parts of a flow chart. One important way in which this symbol is used is to indicate the connections between the main body of a program and its subroutines. Letters are placed in the connector symbols to indicate which connect with which.

The following is a flow chart for Program 7.1.

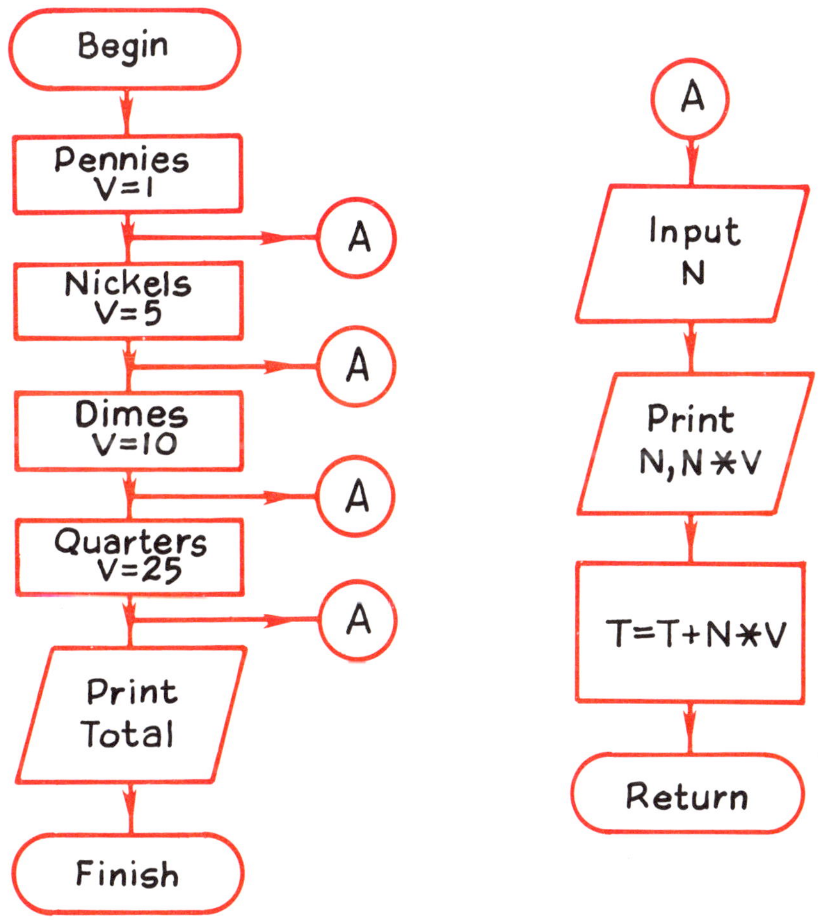

When a connector symbol is encountered in the main program, execution proceeds to the connector bearing the same letter in the subroutine. You should understand that after the RETURN box is reached, execution goes back to the box in the main program which follows the last connector used.

EXERCISES

PART A

1. Have the computer produce the printout below. Include a subroutine that prints each blank line and its following line.

```
]RUN

PART 1
****************************************

PART 2
!               !               !

PART 3
ABABABABABABABABABABABAJABABABABABABABAB
```

2. Rewrite the following program, eliminating ON X entirely and using a subroutine instead.

```
20   PRINT "PRICE, NUMBER OF CEREALS"
30   GOTO 200
40   PRINT "PRICE, NUMBER OF MILKS"
50   GOTO 200
60   PRINT "PRICE, NUMBER OF SWEETENERS"
70   GOTO 200
80   PRINT "TOTAL EXPENSE = $";E
90   PRINT "TOTAL NUMBER OF ITEMS = ";T
100   END
200   INPUT P,N
210 E = E + P * N
220 T = T + N
230 X = X + 1
240   ON X GOTO 40,60,80
```

3. Have the computer pick a random integer from 1 to 4 which will determine whether the prize to be awarded will be a ball, balloon, toy car, or candy bar.

4. Input an integer from 1 to 3. The integer should cause one of the following three fortunes to be printed.

FAME IS YOURS IF NO ONE EATS YOUR APPLE.
BLAME IS YOURS IF SOMEONE BEATS YOUR APPLE.
SUCCESS IS YOURS IF YOU DON'T MISTREAT THE APPLE.

5. Write a flow chart that causes the string A$="1234567890" to be printed four times on the same line. Write the corresponding program based on your flow chart.

6. Dizzy Astor wants to use the computer to input a number X, and then have the computer square X, square the result, square it again, and print the result. Help him by drawing the appropriate flow chart and then the corresponding program.

7. Draw a flow chart for entering a number X, asking for another value if its absolute value is less than 1, taking the INT of the absolute value of X (call the result N), printing the word "REPEAT" N times in a column, and finally printing the word "FINISHED". Write the corresponding program.

8. Lottsmore Trubbel wants to generate a set of twenty numbers greater than zero and less than 100, using a FOR . . . NEXT loop. Only the largest of the set is to be printed. Write a flow chart and its corresponding program for Lottsmore.

9. Draw a flow chart for review question number 1.

10. What is the exact output for the following program?

```
10   READ X
20   ON X GOTO 30,40,50,60,70,80,99
30   PRINT "MERRILY, ";: GOTO 10
40   PRINT "ROW, ";: GOTO 10
50   PRINT "YOUR BOAT": GOTO 10
60   PRINT "GENTLY DOWN THE STREAM": GOTO 10
70   PRINT "LIFE IS BUT A DREAM": GOTO 10
80   PRINT : GOTO 10
90   DATA  2,2,2,3,4,1,1,1,1,6,5,7
99   END
```

11. (a) Give the exact order in which the lines of the following program are executed.
    (b) If line 80 is changed to 80 DATA 3,0,4,-5,-1,-8,1,5,999 what will be the output?

```
10   READ X
20   IF X = 999 THEN 90
30   ON  SGN (X) + 2 GOSUB 50,60,70
40   GOTO 10
50 N = N + 1: RETURN
60 Z = Z + 1: RETURN
70 P = P + 1: RETURN
80   DATA  6,-1,0,999
90   PRINT "N = ";N,"Z = ";Z,"P = ";P
```

12. Flowchart the following program:

```
10   READ A,B
20 L = 2 * A + 2 * B
30   PRINT "PERIMETER IS ";L
40   GOTO 10
50   DATA  5,8,13,21,34,55
```

13. (a) Give the exact order in which the lines of the following program are executed.
(b) If line 90 were changed to 90 DATA 1,8,-2,5,-3,-6,2,4,-7,0, what would the output be?

```
10  READ X
20  IF X = 0 THEN 95
30  GOSUB 60
40 T = T + X
50  GOTO 10
60  IF X < 0 THEN 80
70 P = P + X
80  RETURN
90  DATA  5,2,-9,0,3,5
95  PRINT "T = ";T,"P = ";P
```

14. Write a program which asks for the dimensions of a triangle and prints its area and perimeter if it is a right triangle. The program should call on a subroutine to check whether the triangle is right or not.

15. Let X and Y be the coordinates of a point in a plane. Write a program which randomly picks X and Y, each as an integer from –5 to 5, inclusive. The user of the program is to guess X and Y, with the guesses being called X1 and Y1. A subroutine must be used to print the distance between the guessed point and the actual point after each guess. The user is to be given 3 guesses and, if unsuccessful, is then to be given the value of X as well as 2 more tries to guess Y.

16. Frequently a flow chart represents an entire subroutine as a single processing or I/O block. Using the following flow chart, write a program which computes averages. Data should be:

3,87,72,93
3,81,86,90
4,95,97,83,89
5,88,92,85,84,91

```
]RUN
NUMBER          SUM             MEAN
3               257             84
3               257             85.6666667
4               364             91
5               440             88
```

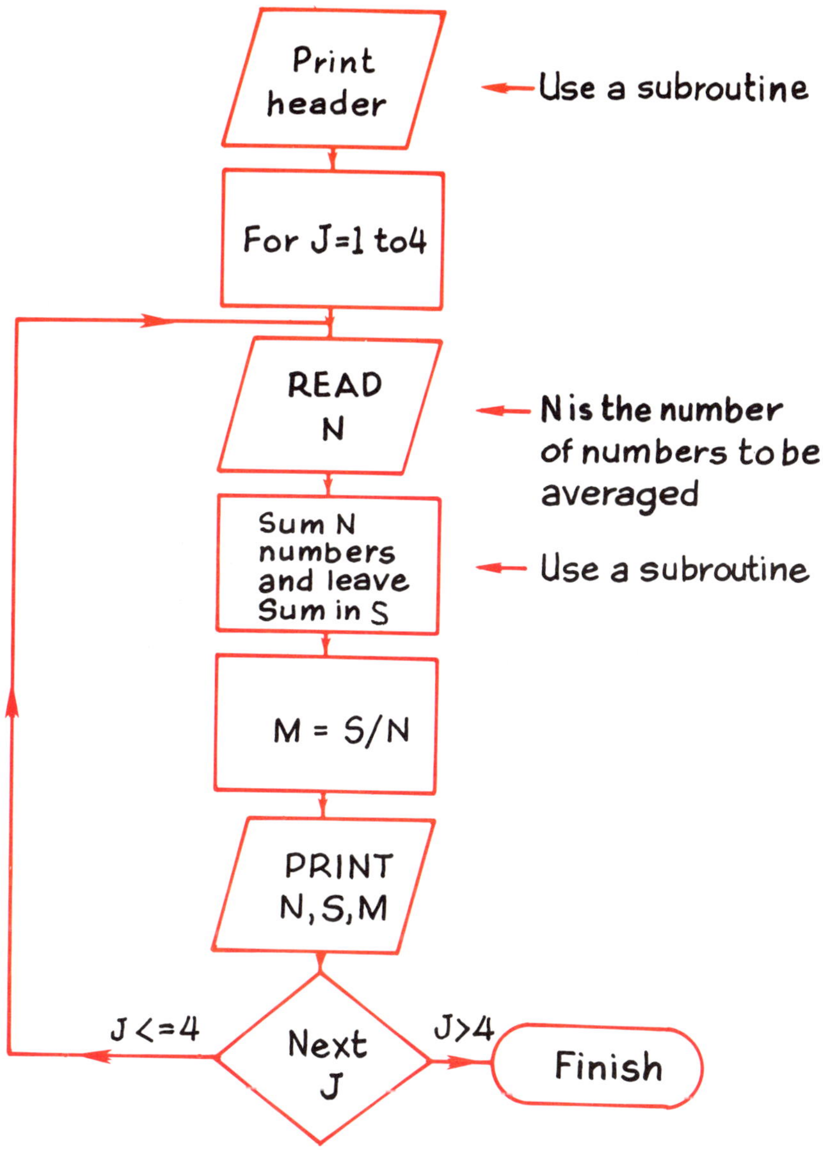
Print header
Use a subroutine
For J=1 to4
READ N
N is the number of numbers to be averaged
Sum N numbers and leave Sum in S
Use a subroutine
M = S/N
PRINT N,S,M
Next J
J<=4
J>4
Finish

17. Isolated in his ski-lodge in the Swiss Alps, Bjorn Rich often gets his mail late. As a result the statements from his Swiss bank account rarely arrive on time. To solve this problem, write a program to assist Bjorn in keeping his account up to date. Have three subroutines which take care of deposits, withdrawals, and interest (compiled quarterly).

18. Peter Kolodnigork has not learned how to write flow charts and has produced the following disaster. It is supposed to be a flow chart for a program which decides whether a number is greater or less than six. If you know more than Peter, correct his flow chart.

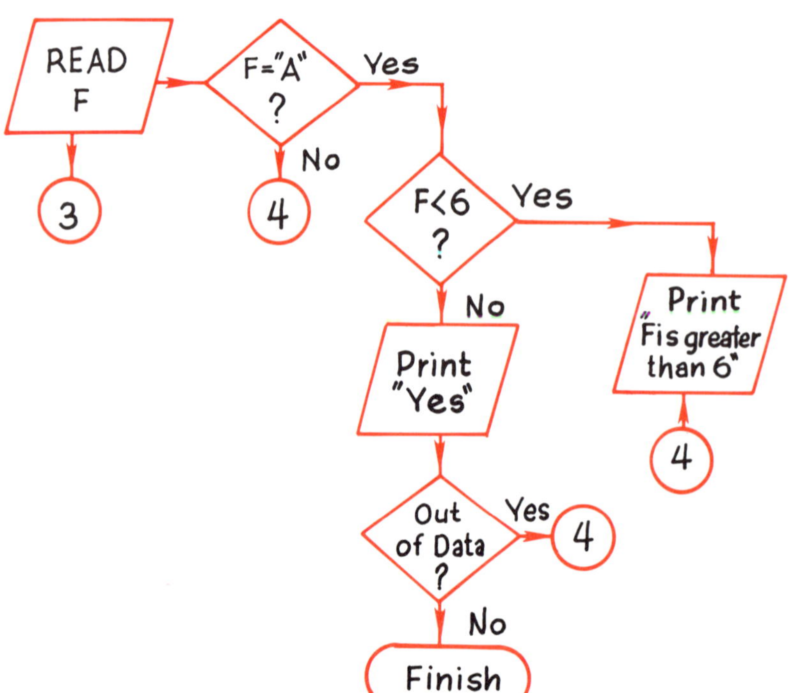

19. The area of any triangle may be found from Hero's formula: Area = $\sqrt{S(S-A)(S-B)(S-C)}$ where A, B, and C are the length of the sides of the triangle and S is the semiperimeter $S = (A + B + C)/2$. Draw a flow chart to calculate the area, given the sides. Write a program based upon the chart.

20. Write a program from the following flow chart:

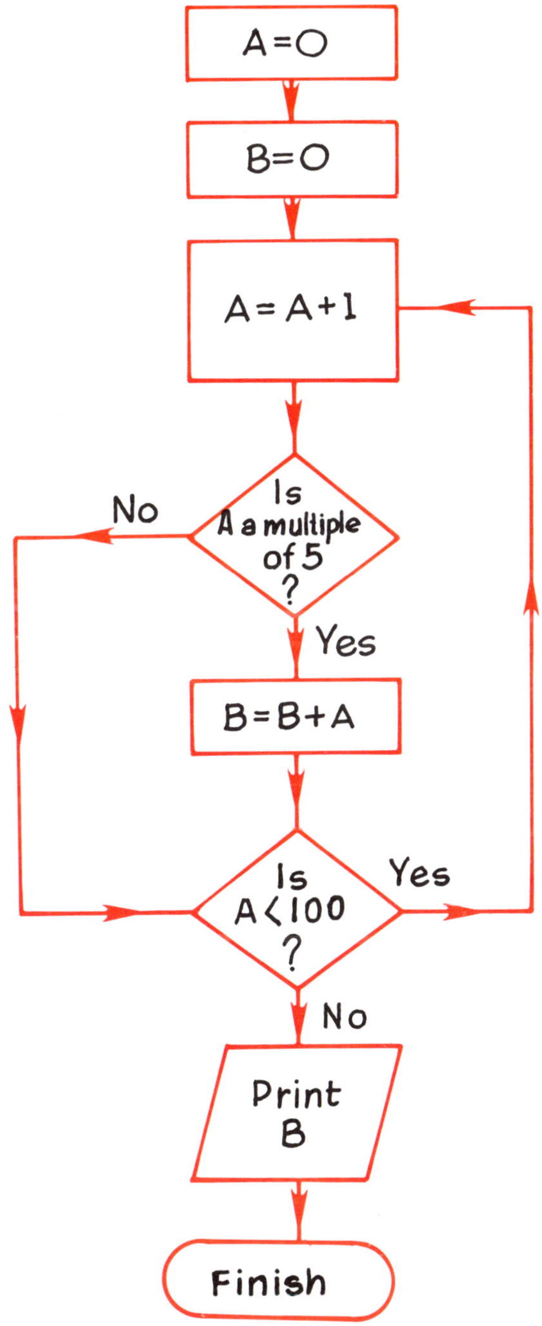

21. Write a program that prints each of the following sentences. Using a subroutine, have only the word APPLE flash in each sentence.

AN APPLE A DAY KEEPS THE DOCTOR AWAY.
IS THERE A BUG IN YOUR APPLE?
HOW DO YOU LIKE THEM APPLES?!
DON'T LET YOUR APPLE ROT!

8

DISK OPERATING SYSTEM

A computer file is similar to a filing cabinet in which information is placed so that it may be recalled and cross-referenced. It provides a means for storing large quantities of data for long periods of time. The APPLE stores files and programs on diskettes.

The APPLE can utilize two different file types: sequential and random-access. The sequential file is best adapted to situations in which the stored data is to be recalled in the same order as it was originally stored in the file. Proceeding line-by-line from the beginning, the computer scans the file until all the desired information is located. If information is to be retrieved from an arbitrary location in the file, the random-access file is to be preferred. Since the random-access file is more difficult to use, sequential files will be explained first.

We suggest that before proceeding to learn the use of files, you first read Appendix B in order to become familiar with the operation of the APPLE disk drives.

Accessing the File

All commands referring to the operation of the disk drives are part of the Disk Operating System (DOS). Several of these commands can be used in the immediate mode, and most of them can be used in a program. To execute a DOS command in a program, a PRINT statement must be used. PRINT must be followed by CTRL-D and then by the command enclosed in quotation marks. For example,

```
10 PRINT "CATALOG"
```

will produce a catalog of the programs and files on the disk in the drive. A CTRL-D is entered into the computer by simultaneously pressing the CTRL and D keys; it is not printed.

Because CTRL characters are not printed, it is often difficult to read a program that has CTRL characters embedded in PRINT statements. The following technique makes obvious the presence of CTRL-D.

```
10 DOS$ = CHR$(4): REM CTRL-D
20 PRINT DOS$;"CATALOG"
```

Assigning CHR$(4) to DOS$ makes DOS$ equal to a CTRL-D. See Chapter 9 for a discussion of CHR$. Whenever the computer detects a CTRL-D at the beginning of a PRINT statement, it recognizes that whatever comes next is to be treated as a DOS command. If it does not constitute a valid DOS command, the message ?SYNTAX ERROR will be displayed, and the program will stop. If the PRINT has a valid DOS command, it will be executed rather than printed on the screen. If there is no CTRL-D at the beginning of the PRINT statement, the DOS command will not be executed but will simply be printed on the screen.

PROGRAM 8.1

This program shows how a DOS command is affected by the presence or absence of CTRL-D.

```
10 DOS$ =  CHR$ (4)
20  PRINT "CATALOG": REM  NO CTRL-D
30  PRINT DOS$;"CATALOG"

]RUN
CATALOG


DISK VOLUME 081

 A 006 BOOT3.3+L&
*I 006 APPLESOFT
*B 050 FPBASIC
*B 050 INTBASIC
*A 002 TURNKEY
*B 010 L&.2K PLUS
 A 055 DATABASE
*B 047 SARGON II
 B 026 TED-B
```

OPEN

The OPEN command instructs the computer to open a file on the disk and ready it for use. For example,

```
10 DOS$ = CHR$ (4)
20 PRINT DOS$;"OPEN MARKS"
```

directs the computer to search for a file named MARKS. If it is not located, the new name is entered in the list of files on the disk after which data can then be entered in the file. If, however, the file MARKS already exists, the computer will use it as a source of data. Since both programs and files can be stored on the disk, different names must be used for each program and file. For example, a program named AVERAGE could be used to access a file named MARKS. So as to avoid using a name twice, you should keep a record of the names of all programs and files.

CLOSE

Any file that has been opened must be closed. To close a file, the command CLOSE is used, followed by the name of the file. For example,

```
50 PRINT DOS$;"CLOSE MARKS"
```

closes the file MARKS. The CLOSE statement ensures that all information for a file is properly retained.

If a program is halted with a CTRL-C or if it encounters an error and stops while a file is open, the file must be closed in the immediate mode. For example,

```
PRINT CHR$ (4);"CLOSE MARKS"
```

WRITE

An OPEN statement merely establishes a line of communication between a program and a file. The WRITE command enables the user to place data in the file. For example,

```
30 DOS$ = CHR$ (4)
35 PRINT DOS$;"OPEN GRADES"
40 PRINT DOS$;"WRITE GRADES"
```

causes all PRINT statements after line 40 to send information to the file instead of to the screen, until the file is closed or another DOS command is executed.

PROGRAM 8.2

This sample program opens a sequential file named WORK which stores the names, hourly wages and number of hours worked by four employees.

```
10 DOS$ =  CHR$ (4)
20  FOR X = 1 TO 4
30  INPUT "NAME? ";N$(X)
40  INPUT "WAGE? ";W(X)
50  INPUT "HOURS WORKED? ";H(X)
60  PRINT
70  NEXT X
80  PRINT DOS$;"OPEN WORK"
90  PRINT DOS$;"WRITE WORK"
100  FOR J = 1 TO 4
110  PRINT N$(J)
120  PRINT W(J)
130  PRINT H(J)
140  NEXT J
150  PRINT DOS$;"CLOSE WORK"
160  PRINT "THE INFORMATION IS IN THE FILE."
```

```
]RUN
NAME? GEORGE MURDOCK
WAGE? 4.45
HOURS WORKED? 39

NAME? JULIE COOK
WAGE? 4.75
HOURS WORKED? 42

NAME? STANLEY MARCUS
WAGE? 5.10
HOURS WORKED? 36.75

NAME? VERA LIND
WAGE? 4.95
HOURS WORKED? 27.5

THE INFORMATION IS IN THE FILE.
```

Note that the PRINT statements in lines 80 and 90 do not cause printing on the screen. The CHR$ (4) at the beginning of each of these two PRINT statements identifies the rest of each statement as a DOS command. The contents of the PRINT statements in lines 110 to 130 do not appear on the screen because the WRITE command in line 90 has instructed the computer to send all subsequent data from PRINT statements to the file WORK. Note that, following the WRITE command at line 90, the PRINT statements should not contain the DOS$ command because they are sending information to the file but are not themselves DOS commands.

Before executing the WRITE command we should input all of the information to be written into a file. If an INPUT statement is executed after a WRITE command, the WRITE command will send the (?) from the INPUT statement to the file instead of to the screen, thus ruining data in the file. To avoid this, all of the information to be put in a file can be stored in subscripted variables by the program prior to the WRITE command.

READ

After a READ command, an INPUT statement takes information from the file instead of the keyboard. For example, if the file WORK exists, the lines

```
25 DOS$ = CHR$ (4)
30 PRINT DOS$;"OPEN WORK"
35 PRINT DOS$;"READ WORK"
```

cause the computer to take information from the file when an INPUT statement occurs. If WORK does not exist, the computer will expect data to be input from the keyboard.

PROGRAM 8.3

This program will open the file WORK created in Program 8.2 and print the names and hours worked for the four employees.

```
10 DOS$ =  CHR$ (4)
20  PRINT "NAME"; TAB( 25);
30  PRINT "HOURS WORKED"
40  PRINT DOS$;"OPEN WORK"
50  PRINT DOS$;"READ WORK"
60  FOR N = 1 TO 4
70  INPUT N$
80  INPUT W
90  INPUT H
100  PRINT N$; TAB( 30);
110  PRINT H
120  NEXT N
130  PRINT DOS$;"CLOSE WORK"
```

```
]RUN
NAME                        HOURS WORKED
GEORGE MURDOCK               39
JULIE COOK                   42
STANLEY MARCUS               36.75
VERA LIND                    27.5
```

The data in the file WORK looks like this.

GEORGE MURDOCK
4.45
39
JULIE COOK
4.75
42
STANLEY MARCUS
5.10
36.75
VERA LIND
4.95
27.5

The computer has a pointer that indicates the next piece of information that is to be transferred from the file by the INPUT statement. As a file is opened, the pointer is placed at the beginning of the file. For example, at line 70 in PROGRAM 8.3 the first item that the computer reads from the file is George Murdock for the variable N$, next it reads 4.45 for the variable W, and then 39 for the variable H. Every time INPUT is encountered, the pointer is advanced to the next item of data in the file. If line 80 were not in the program, 4.45 would be read for George Murdock's hours. The next time through the loop, 39 would be put in N$ and Julie Cook in H. The latter operation would cause the computer to generate an error message. It is vital for a programmer to remember the structure of a sequential file and to use INPUT statements accordingly. Notice that at line 80 the wage was input, even though it was not printed in the program. This was necessary in order to keep the computer reading the file in the correct sequence.

APPEND

APPEND gives the programmer the ability to add information to an already existing sequential file by adding the new information after that which has been previously stored. For example,

```
15 DOS$ = CHR$ (4)
20 PRINT DOS$;"APPEND WORK"
25 PRINT DOS$;"WRITE WORK"
```

The APPEND command is used at line 20 instead of the OPEN command. When an OPEN command is executed, the computer opens the specified file and either prepares to read from it or write into it, starting at the beginning of the file. If the programmer adds additional information to an old file, the new information will be written over the old at the beginning of the file, and in the process, will thus destroy the old information. To avoid this erasure, the APPEND command opens an old file and prepares the computer to write new information at the end.

PROGRAM 8.4

This program will update the old WORK file created in Program 8.2 to enable it to include information on two new employees just hired.

```
10 DOS$ =  CHR$ (4)
20  FOR Q = 1 TO 2
30  INPUT "NAME? ";N$(Q)
40  INPUT "WAGE? ";W(Q)
50  INPUT "HOURS WORKED? ";H(Q)
60  PRINT
70  NEXT Q
80  PRINT DOS$;"APPEND WORK"
90  PRINT DOS$;"WRITE WORK"
100  FOR T = 1 TO 2
110  PRINT N$(T)
120  PRINT W(T)
130  PRINT H(T)
140  NEXT T
150  PRINT DOS$;"CLOSE WORK"
160  PRINT "THE FILE HAS BEEN UPDATED"

]RUN
NAME? JOHN MORAN
WAGE? 4.60
HOURS WORKED? 44.25

NAME? REBECCA SWAYNE
WAGE? 4.80
HOURS WORKED? 41.5

THE FILE HAS BEEN UPDATED
```

The APPEND command must always be followed by a WRITE command. If a READ command is executed after an APPEND, the computer will look for data past the end of the file and this process will generate an error.

There is no single command that will remove unwanted information from a sequential file. To change a file we must transfer its information to a new one. After transferring the wanted information, we can destroy the old file by using the DELETE command. By using the RENAME command we rename the newly created file with the name of the old one.

PROGRAM 8.5

When an employee retires, this program will remove the employee's name from the file WORK.

```
10 DOS$ =  CHR$ (4)
20  INPUT "WHO HAS RETIRED? ";R$
30  PRINT DOS$;"OPEN WORK"
40  PRINT DOS$;"OPEN TEMPORARY"
50  FOR X = 1 TO 6
60  PRINT DOS$;"READ WORK"
70  INPUT N$
80  INPUT W
90  INPUT H
100  IF N$ = R$ THEN 150
110  PRINT DOS$;"WRITE TEMPORARY"
120  PRINT N$
130  PRINT W
140  PRINT H
150  NEXT X
160  PRINT DOS$;"CLOSE WORK"
170  PRINT DOS$;"CLOSE TEMPORARY"
180  PRINT DOS$;"DELETE WORK"
190  PRINT DOS$;"RENAME TEMPORARY, WORK"
200  PRINT "THE INFORMATION ON ";R$
210  PRINT "HAS BEEN REMOVED."

]RUN
WHO HAS RETIRED? VERA LIND
THE INFORMATION ON VERA LIND
HAS BEEN REMOVED.
```

Program 8.5 reads all the information in the file WORK. Line 100 waits until the name of the retired employee is read and then skips that person. The information on all the other employees is placed in the new file TEMPORARY. When this is complete, the old file WORK is destroyed at line 180. Then the file TEMPORARY is given the name WORK at line 190. See Appendix B for an explanation of DELETE and RENAME. The new WORK file contains all the data from the old one except the information on the person who retired.

This program works well for this limited example, but the technique it uses is not always practical. The FOR . . . NEXT loop between lines 50 and 150 prevents the program from attempting to read data past the end of the file. This method was used because the length of the file WORK was known. If the length of a file is not known, a FOR . . . NEXT loop cannot be employed. Instead, the GOTO statement must be used to ensure a reading of the complete file. The entire file will then be read until the computer comes to the file's end. At this point an OUT OF DATA error will occur, and the program will be halted. In this instance, files will be left open, and important data may be lost. To prevent the computer from stopping when an error is encountered, the ONERR GOTO statement is used.

ONERR GOTO and RESUME

The ONERR GOTO statement tells the computer what it must do when an error is encountered. For example,

15 ONERR GOTO 375

If an error occurs after this statement, the computer goes to the line specified. It is important to place an ONERR GOTO statement early in a program so that the computer takes note of it before an error occurs.

PROGRAM 8.6

This program is a revision of Program 8.5 that allows the file WORK to be of any length.

```
10  ONERR  GOTO 190
20 DOS$ =  CHR$ (4)
30 T = 0
40  INPUT "WHO HAS RETIRED? ";R$
50  PRINT DOS$;"OPEN WORK"
60  PRINT DOS$;"OPEN TEMPORARY"
70  PRINT DOS$;"READ WORK"
80  INPUT N$
90  INPUT W
100  INPUT H
110  IF N$ = R$ THEN 170
120  PRINT DOS$;"WRITE TEMPORARY"
130  PRINT N$
140  PRINT W
150  PRINT H
160  GOTO 70
170 T = 1
180  GOTO 80
190  PRINT DOS$;"CLOSE WORK"
200  PRINT DOS$;"CLOSE TEMPORARY"
210  PRINT
220  IF T = 1 THEN 270
230  PRINT DOS$;"DELETE TEMPORARY"
240  PRINT "THERE IS NO ";R$
250  PRINT "ON THE PAYROLL"
260  END
270  PRINT DOS$;"DELETE WORK"
280  PRINT DOS$;"RENAME TEMPORARY, WORK"
290  PRINT R$;" HAS BEEN TAKEN"
300  PRINT "OFF THE PAYROLL"

]RUN
WHO HAS RETIRED? SANDRA COOK

THERE IS NO SANDRA COOK
ON THE PAYROLL
```

Program 8.6 shows two major improvements over Program 8.5. Program 8.6 tells the user if a name has been entered that is not in the file. It also utilizes the ONERR GOTO and a GOTO loop to read the entire file. Note that the variable T is used to indicate whether the name being sought is in the file. If this be the case, T becomes 1; if not, it remains 0. This technique is recommended for reading any sequential file.

Once an error has been trapped, the statement RESUME will send the APPLE to the line where the error occurred. If conditions have not changed, the error will recur and be trapped again, thus making the APPLE go around in an infinte loop. If conditions are changed by the error trap, program execution will continue from the line where the error had originally occurred.

The following programs illustrate applications for the use of the material covered in this chapter. They consist of a series of examples concerning the record keeping process of a sporting goods manufacturer.

PROGRAM 8.7

This program will produce a file that contains the sales records of all salesmen working for the Acme Sporting Goods Company. Each salesman sells baseball bats, balls, and helmets.

```
10 DOS$ =  CHR$ (4)
20  INPUT "HOW MANY SALESPERSONS DO YOU HAVE? ";P
30  DIM NM$(P),BT(P),BL(P),HT(P)
40  FOR E = 1 TO P
50  INPUT "SALESPERSON? ";NM$(E)
60  INPUT "BATS SOLD? ";BT(E)
70  INPUT "BALLS SOLD? ";BL(E)
80  INPUT "HELMETS SOLD? ";HT(E)
85  PRINT
90  NEXT E
100  PRINT DOS$;"OPEN SALES RECORDS"
110  PRINT DOS$;"WRITE SALES RECORDS"
120  FOR Q = 1 TO P
130  PRINT NM$(Q)
140  PRINT BT(Q)
150  PRINT BL(Q)
160  PRINT HT(Q)
170  NEXT Q
180  PRINT DOS$;"CLOSE SALES RECORDS"
190  PRINT "THE INFORMATION IS IN THE FILE."

]RUN
HOW MANY SALESPERSONS DO YOU HAVE? 5
SALESPERSON? JOSEPH GREER
BATS SOLD? 32
BALLS SOLD? 17
HELMETS SOLD? 23

SALESPERSON? DON KIDDER
BATS SOLD? 4
BALLS SOLD? 10
HELMETS SOLD? 5

SALESPERSON? FIONA L'HUILLIER
BATS SOLD? 29
BALLS SOLD? 34
HELMETS SOLD? 52

SALESPERSON? ROBERT OAKLEY
BATS SOLD? 45
BALLS SOLD? 17
HELMETS SOLD? 39

SALESPERSON? CYNTHIA GARFIELD
BATS SOLD? 26
BALLS SOLD? 32
HELMETS SOLD? 12

THE INFORMATION IS IN THE FILE.
```

PROGRAM 8.8

This program will update the sales records for an individual salesman.

```
10  ONERR  GOTO 220
20 DOS$ =  CHR$ (4)
30  INPUT "WHOSE SALES HAVE CHANGED? ";C$
40  PRINT DOS$;"OPEN SALES RECORDS"
50  PRINT DOS$;"OPEN TEMPORARY"
60  PRINT DOS$;"READ SALES RECORDS"
70  INPUT NM$
80  INPUT BT
90  INPUT BL
100  INPUT HT
110  IF NM$ = C$ THEN 180
120  PRINT DOS$;"WRITE TEMPORARY"
130  PRINT NM$
140  PRINT BT
150  PRINT BL
160  PRINT HT
170  GOTO 60
180  PRINT DOS$
185  INPUT "BATS SOLD? ";BT
190  INPUT "BALLS SOLD? ";BL
200  INPUT "HELMETS SOLD? ";HT
210  GOTO 120
220  PRINT DOS$;"CLOSE SALES RECORDS"
230  PRINT DOS$;"CLOSE TEMPORARY"
240  PRINT DOS$;"DELETE SALES RECORDS"
250  PRINT DOS$;"RENAME TEMPORARY, SALES RECORDS"
260  PRINT
270  PRINT C$;"'S RECORDS"
280  PRINT "HAVE BEEN UPDATED"

]RUN
WHOSE SALES HAVE CHANGED? CYNTHIA GARFIELD
BATS SOLD? 30
BALLS SOLD? 38
HELMETS SOLD? 22

CYNTHIA GARFIELD'S RECORDS
HAVE BEEN UPDATED
```

Note that line 180 is required to cancel the READ statement of line 60, thereby allowing the inputs of lines 185-200 to come from the keyboard.

PROGRAM 8.9

This program will write a personalized letter of congratulations to all salespersons who have sold 75 units or more.

```
10  ONERR  GOTO 220
20  PRINT
30 T = 0
40 DOS$ =  CHR$ (4)
50  PRINT DOS$;"OPEN SALES RECORDS"
60  PRINT DOS$;"READ SALES RECORDS"
70  INPUT NM$
80  INPUT BT
90  INPUT BL
100  INPUT HT
110  IF BT + BL + HT >  = 75 GOTO 130
120  GOTO 70
130 T = T + 1
140  PRINT "DEAR ";NM$
150  PRINT "     CONGRATULATIONS, YOU ARE"
160  PRINT "ONE OF OUR TOP SALESPERSONS.  YOUR"
170  PRINT "BONUS CHECK IS IN THE MAIL."
180  PRINT
190  PRINT "                        YOUR BOSS"
200  PRINT : PRINT : PRINT
210  GOTO 70
220  PRINT DOS$;"CLOSE SALES RECORDS"
230  IF T = 0 GOTO 260
240  PRINT T;" SALESPERSONS WILL RECIEVE A BONUS."
250  END
260  PRINT "NO ONE SOLD ENOUGH."
270  PRINT "TELL THEM TO TRY HARDER."

]RUN

DEAR FIONA L'HUILLIER
     CONGRATULATIONS, YOU ARE
ONE OF OUR TOP SALESPERSONS.  YOUR
BONUS CHECK IS IN THE MAIL.

                        YOUR BOSS


DEAR ROBERT OAKLEY
     CONGRATULATIONS, YOU ARE
ONE OF OUR TOP SALESPERSONS.  YOUR
BONUS CHECK IS IN THE MAIL.

                        YOUR BOSS


DEAR CYNTHIA GARFIELD
     CONGRATULATIONS, YOU ARE
ONE OF OUR TOP SALESPERSONS.  YOUR
BONUS CHECK IS IN THE MAIL.

                        YOUR BOSS



3 SALESPERSONS WILL RECIEVE A BONUS.
```

Random-Access Files

A random-access file is structured like a collection of drawers, each of which may be accessed individually. This filing system is obviously superior to the one drawer file structure of a sequential file. To read the last piece of data in a sequential file, every piece of data preceding it must be read in sequence. Yet, to read the last piece of data in a random-access file only the last "drawer" needs to be opened. In the APPLE each "drawer" is called a record, and it consists of space reserved to store information. The length of a record, i.e., the number of characters it can hold, is specified when a random-access file is created. The records in a file can be short or long, but they must all be of the same length. A single record need not hold just one item. It can hold as many strings and/or numbers as needed as long as the total number of characters does not exceed the specified length of the record.

OPEN

Random-access files use the OPEN statement. The length of the records in the file must be specified by an L for length, which is followed by the number of characters in the record.

The example below will create a random-access file named KAZOO, with each record in the file being fifty characters long. Each time a random-access file is opened, it is important to specify the length of the records in the file. Otherwise, data will not be read from the file or placed in it correctly.

```
20 PRINT DOS$;"OPEN KAZOO, L50"
```

WRITE

When used by random-access files, the WRITE command sends information to a specific record of the file. For example,

```
40 PRINT DOS$;"WRITE JONES,R";A
```

sends information to record number A in the file JONES. Note that it is necessary to follow the file name with a comma and the letter R (for random-access).

PROGRAM 8.10

This program will create the file ADDRESS and will put names and addresses for five people in the file.

```
10 DOS$ =  CHR$ (4)
20  PRINT DOS$;"OPEN ADDRESS,L35"
30  FOR X = 1 TO 5
40  INPUT "NAME? ";N$(X)
50  INPUT "STREET ADDRESS? ";A$(X)
60  PRINT
70  NEXT X
80  FOR Q = 1 TO 5
90  PRINT DOS$;"WRITE ADDRESS,R";Q
100  PRINT N$(Q)
110  PRINT A$(Q)
120  NEXT Q
130  PRINT DOS$;"CLOSE ADDRESS"
140  PRINT "THE INFORMATION IS IN THE FILE."

]RUN
NAME? C. MAHAN
STREET ADDRESS? 186 BLUE SPRUCE DR.

NAME? G. MANDEL
STREET ADDRESS? 338 OPOSSUM AVE.

NAME? R. MACPHERSON
STREET ADDRESS? 116 FRANKLIN CORNER ROAD

NAME? C. JENKINS
STREET ADDRESS? 12 NEWPORT RD.

NAME? D. RIMMER
STREET ADDRESS? 1 SANDBURG DR.

THE INFORMATION IS IN THE FILE.
```

At line 80 the variable Q specifies the number of the record in which each name and address is to be placed.

The random-access file is structured as follows, with each record containing an N$(Q) and an A$(Q).

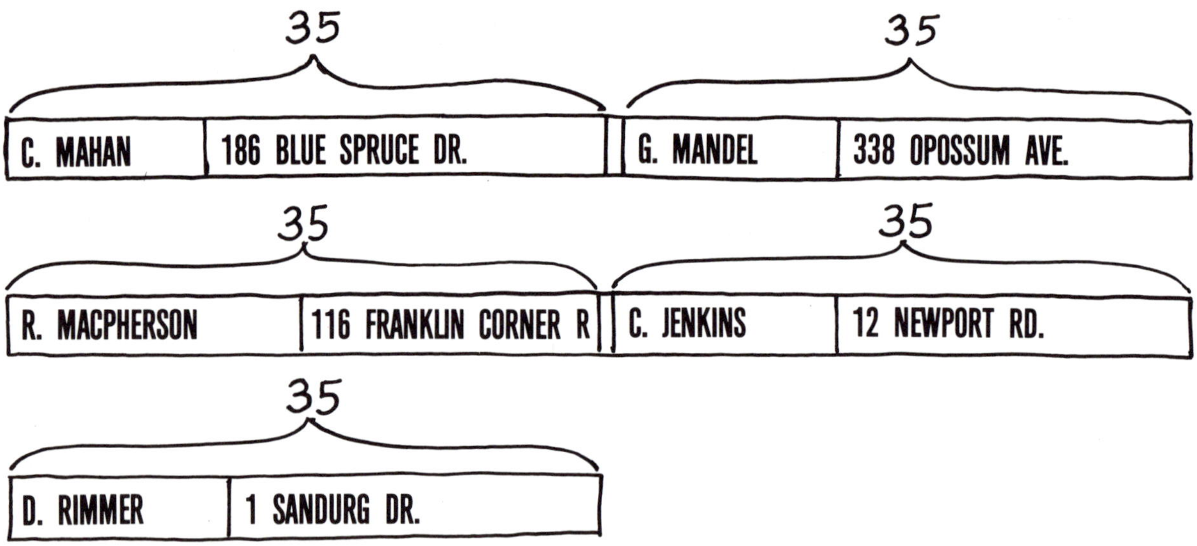

Each record is 35 spaces long, even though the data in the record may take up less than 35 spaces. Note that an attempt was made to enter more than 35 characters in the third record with the result that the characters after the 35th were lost. A blank counts as a character.

READ

Random-access files require us to specify the location of the record to be read. For example,

```
40 PRINT DOS$;"READ ADDRESS,R";A
```

will direct the computer to input from record A at the next INPUT statement. It is this ability to select a specific record that makes random-access files more efficient to use than sequential files.

PROGRAM 8.11

This program will retrieve the name and address stored in any record of the file ADDRESS.

```
10  ONERR  GOTO 90
20 DOS$ =  CHR$ (4)
30  PRINT "ENTER A NEGATIVE NUMBER"
35  PRINT "TO STOP THE PROGRAM."
37  PRINT DOS$;"OPEN ADDRESS,L35"
40  INPUT "WHICH RECORD? ";I
45  IF I < 0 GOTO 110
50  PRINT DOS$;"READ ADDRESS,R";I
60  INPUT N$: INPUT A$
70  PRINT N$: PRINT A$
80  PRINT DOS$: PRINT
85  GOTO 40
90  PRINT "THE FILE IS NOT THAT LONG."
100  GOTO 37
110  PRINT DOS$;"CLOSE ADDRESS"
```

```
]RUN
ENTER A NEGATIVE NUMBER
TO STOP THE PROGRAM.
WHICH RECORD? 1
C. MAHAN
186 BLUE SPRUCE DR.

WHICH RECORD? 3
R. MACPHERSON
116 FRANKLIN CORNER RC. JENKINS

WHICH RECORD? -1
```

The entering of a negative number at line 40 will direct the computer to line 110 and close the file. The error trap at line 10 is employed to inform the user if a record number past the end of the file has been specified without allowing the error to stop the program.

Note that in Program 8.10 an attempt was made to enter more than 35 characters into the third record. This caused the beginning of the fourth record to be joined to the end of the third, and thus to be printed with it. It is very important that no attempt be made to use more than the allotted space in a record.

The lone CTRL-D at line 80 cancels the READ executed at line 50 so that the INPUT at line 40 will request data from the keyboard and not use data from the file.

The following series of programs establishes a file named GRADES which contains the names and grades of a number of students and then demonstrates how the file can be used.

PROGRAM 8.12

This program will store student's names and grades for four courses. In each case the student's I.D. number is used as the record number.

```
10 DOS$ =  CHR$ (4)
20  INPUT "HOW MANY STUDENTS? ";S
30  DIM N$(S),C1(S),C2(S),C3(S),C4(S)
40  FOR I = 1 TO S
50  PRINT "STUDENT #";I;
60  INPUT N$(I)
70  INPUT "FIRST COURSE? ";C1(I)
80  INPUT "SECOND COURSE? ";C2(I)
90  INPUT "THIRD COURSE? ";C3(I)
100  INPUT "FOURTH COURSE? ";C4(I)
110  PRINT
120  NEXT I
130  PRINT DOS$;"OPEN GRADES,L40"
140  FOR Q = 1 TO S
150  PRINT DOS$;"WRITE GRADES,R";Q
160  PRINT N$(Q)
170  PRINT C1(Q)
180  PRINT C2(Q)
190  PRINT C3(Q)
200  PRINT C4(Q)
210  NEXT Q
220  PRINT DOS$;"CLOSE GRADES"
230  PRINT "THE INFORMATION IS IN THE FILE."
```

```
]RUN
HOW MANY STUDENTS? 3
STUDENT #1?ELI HUROWITZ
FIRST COURSE? 82
SECOND COURSE? 79
THIRD COURSE? 75
FOURTH COURSE? 80

STUDENT #2?KIM BAILY
FIRST COURSE? 76
SECOND COURSE? 81
THIRD COURSE? 75
FOURTH COURSE? 78

STUDENT #3?DOUG PATRICK
FIRST COURSE? 85
SECOND COURSE? 87
THIRD COURSE? 82
FOURTH COURSE? 91

THE INFORMATION IS IN THE FILE.
```

Because fewer than 10 elements of data were used in the preceding programs the subscripted variables were not dimensioned. The DIM statement in line 30 allows for any number of students.

PROGRAM 8.13

This program will read a particular student's grades and print them next to the computed average.

```
10  ONERR  GOTO 170
20 DOS$ =  CHR$ (4)
30  PRINT "ENTER A NEGATIVE NUMBER"
40  PRINT "TO STOP THE PROGRAM."
50  PRINT DOS$;"OPEN GRADES,L40"
60  PRINT
70  INPUT "STUDENT'S I.D.#? ";ID
80  IF ID < 0 THEN 190
90  PRINT DOS$;"READ GRADES,R";ID
100  INPUT N$: INPUT C1
110  INPUT C2: INPUT C3
120  INPUT C4: PRINT N$
130  PRINT C1; TAB( 7);C2; TAB( 14);C3; TAB( 21);
140  PRINT C4; TAB( 28);(C1 + C2 + C3 + C4) / 4
150  PRINT DOS$
160  GOTO 60
170  PRINT "THERE IS NO STUDENT WITH THAT NUMBER."
180  GOTO 150
190  PRINT DOS$;"CLOSE GRADES"
```

```
]RUN
ENTER A NEGATIVE NUMBER
TO STOP THE PROGRAM.

STUDENT'S I.D.#? 2
KIM BAILY
76     81      75      78      77.5

STUDENT'S I.D.#? 5
THERE IS NO STUDENT WITH THAT NUMBER.

STUDENT'S I.D.#? 1
ELI HUROWITZ
82     79      75      80      79

STUDENT'S I.D.#? -1
```

PROGRAM 8.14

This program will allow a teacher to correct a mistake in a student's grade report.

```
10  ONERR  GOTO 230
20 DOS$ =  CHR$ (4)
30  PRINT "ENTER A NEGATIVE NUMBER TO STOP."
40  PRINT DOS$;"OPEN GRADES,L40"
50  INPUT "STUDENT I.D.? ";ID
60  IF ID < 0 THEN 250
70  PRINT DOS$;"READ GRADES,R";ID
80  INPUT N$: INPUT C1
90  INPUT C2: INPUT C3
110  INPUT C4: PRINT DOS$
120  PRINT "C1=";C1;"  C2=";C2;"  C3=";C3;"  C4=";C4
130  PRINT "ENTER NEW GRADES."
140  INPUT "FIRST COURSE? ";C1
150  INPUT "SECOND COURSE? ";C2
160  INPUT "THIRD COURSE? ";C3
170  INPUT "FOURTH COURSE? ";C4
180  PRINT DOS$;"WRITE GRADES,R";ID
190  PRINT N$: PRINT C1
200  PRINT C2: PRINT C3
210  PRINT C4: PRINT DOS$
220  PRINT N$;"'S RECORDS ARE UPDATED.": GOTO 50
230  PRINT "THERE IS NO STUDENT WITH THAT NUMBER."
240  GOTO 50
250  PRINT DOS$;"CLOSE GRADES"

]RUN
ENTER A NEGATIVE NUMBER TO STOP.
STUDENT I.D.? 2
C1=76  C2=81  C3=75  C4=78
ENTER NEW GRADES.
FIRST COURSE? 76
SECOND COURSE? 81
THIRD COURSE? 85
FOURTH COURSE? 78
KIM BAILY'S RECORDS ARE UPDATED.
STUDENT I.D.? -1
```

Lines 110 and 210 have CTRL-D's without any DOS commands. The CTRL-D at line 110 cancels the READ executed at line 70 so that the INPUT's from lines 140 to 170 will request information from the keyboard instead of the disk. The CTRL-D in line 210 cancels the WRITE executed at line 180 so that rather than being sent to the file, the message "RECORDS ARE UPDATED" instead appears on the screen.

Accessing Multiple Files

It is possible to open three or more files simultaneously within a single program. When this is done it is important not to confuse the variable associated with each specific file. To open more than three files the command

MAXFILES N

is used where N is the number of files to be opened. The maximum value of N is 16. Opening a large number of files within one program may result in exceeding the Apple's memory range.

PROGRAM 8.15

The following program creates a random-access file named CURRICULAR which will contain the extra-curricular activities and athletic teams of which students are members. As in PROGRAM 8.14, student I.D. numbers are used to reference information.

```
10 DOS$ =  CHR$ (4)
20  PRINT DOS$;"OPEN CURRICULAR,L35"
30  INPUT "HOW MANY STUDENTS? ";S
40  DIM A$(S),T$(S)
50  FOR X = 1 TO S
60  PRINT"STUDENT#";S
70  INPUT "ACTIVITY? ";A$(X)
80  INPUT "TEAM? ";T$(X)
90  NEXT X
100  FOR Z = 1 TO S
110  PRINT DOS$;"WRITE CURRICULAR,R";Z
120  PRINT A$(Z): PRINT T$(Z)
130  NEXT X
140  PRINT DOS$;"CLOSE CURRICULAR"
150  PRINT "THE INFORMATION IS IN THE FILE."
```

PROGRAM 8.16

The following program opens the files GRADES and CURRICULAR and prints the names and grade averages for each member of the football team.

```
10 DOS$ =  CHR$ (4): ONERR  GOTO 150
20  PRINT DOS$;"OPEN GRADES,L40"
30  PRINT DOS$;"OPEN CURRICULAR,L35"
40 Z = Z + 1
50  PRINT DOS$;"READ CURRICULAR,R";Z
60  INPUT A$: INPUT B$
70  IF T$ = "FOOTBALL" THEN 90
80  GOTO 40
90  PRINT DOS$;"READ GRADES,R";Z
100  INPUT N$: INPUT C1
110  INPUT C2: INPUT C3
120  INPUT C4: PRINT N$,
130  PRINT (C1 + C2 + C3 + C4) / 4
140  GOTO 40
150  PRINT DOS$;"CLOSE GRADES"
160  PRINT DOS$;"CLOSE CURRICULAR"
```

EXERCISES

PART A

1. Store 50 random numbers between 0 and 20 in a sequential file. Use a second program to retrieve the numbers, add them, and print the sum.

2. Store in a sequential file the names and prices of five different desserts served at MADGE'S DINER. With a second program add two additional desserts. Have a third program retrieve and print the information.

3. Store ten different first names of friends in a sequential file. A second program is to print all the names in the file which begin with the letters D,E,F,G, and H or a message if none are found.

4. Store the 26 letters of the alphabet in a random-access file in order. Have a program pick five random numbers from 1 to 26 and use these numbers to put together a five letter "word".

5. Store titles of ten books in a random-access file. Use this file to make a sequential file for all the titles beginning with letters from N to Z, inclusive.

6. Input a number X, and print its square. If an error occurs (e.g. a string is entered) the program should be able to recover.

PART B

7. (a) Create a random-access file named ACCOUNTS that will contain the customer name and current balance for twenty-five savings accounts.
   (b) Write a program that will update the file ACCOUNTS whenever an individual makes a deposit or withdrawal.
   (c) Write a program using the file ACCOUNTS that sends a letter of warning to the holders of all overdrawn accounts or a letter of congratulations to the holders of accounts with $500 or more informing them that they will be receiving a toaster in the mail.

8. (a) Create a random-access file named CARS to record how many full-sized, mid-sized and compact cars a dealer sells each month for a twelve month period.
   (b) Write a program that will retrieve information from the file CARS for a specific month and then print a bar graph comparing the sales of three sizes of cars.

9. (a) Write a program that will create a random-access file FRAT which contains the names, fraternities, and ages of thirty college students.
   (b) Write a program that will access FRAT and create a sequential file SIGMA which contains the names and ages of the students who live in Sigma Chi.
   (c) Write a program that accesses the file FRAT and randomly selects twenty-five students for seats in a classroom of five rows, five seats to a row. Have the computer print a seating plan for the class, placing each student's name at the correct seat location.

10. (a) Two persons, NIT and WIT, measured the Fahrenheit temperature (F) outside on Feb. 12 at various times (T) during a ten hour period. Their results are recorded here. Set up two sequential files, one for each person's data, naming each file after that person.

NIT	T	F	WIT	T	F
	0.0	18.1		1.0	20.9
	2.1	24.0		1.9	23.3
	3.8	27.2		3.5	26.1
	6.0	29.3		6.0	28.8
	8.0	26.6		8.2	26.2
	9.0	16.1		10.0	16.0

(b) Write a program that will merge the two files into one sequential file named MERGE. The times should be sequentially in order. However, when a value of (T) occurs both in NIT and WIT, the average of the two values of (F) should be placed in MERGE.

(c) Retrieve and print the contents of MERGE.

11. (a) Create a sequential payroll file called PAY to store each of ten person's names (last name first), his or her hourly pay rate, the number of dependents, and deductions for medical and life insurance for each week. Supply appropriate data.

(b) Use PAY to prepare the payroll data sheet (supply the number of hours (H) each person worked during the week). The sheet should list the name, hours worked, gross pay, three deductions, and net pay. Assume a tax rate of 25%, with 2% being subtracted from this rate for each dependent.

9 DATA TYPES

Modern computers have resulted from the union of the binary number system with the principles of electricity. The binary number system uses only two digits, 0 and 1, and can therefore be represented by the two states of an electric circuit, off or on. This concept has made digital computers possible, since they operate by reducing all data to a binary code. How different types of data can be reduced to a binary system is explained in this chapter.

Binary Code

The most familiar number system, the decimal system uses ten digits: 0, 1, 2, 3, 4, 5, 6, 7, 8, 9 and is therefore considered to be base ten. In contrast, the binary system, which uses only the digits 0 and 1, is base two.

In the base ten system columns are used to represent powers of ten with the first column left of the decimal point representing 10^0, the second 10^1, the third 10^2, and so on. For example, in the numeral 458, 8 represents 8×10^0, 5 represents 5×10^1, and 4 represents 4×10^2. The numeral itself represents the sum: $4 \times 10^2 + 5 \times 10^1 + 8 \times 10^0$.

The base two system works identically *except that columns represent powers of two* instead of ten. For example, in the numeral 101, the 1 on the right represents 1×2^0, the 0 represents 0×2^1, and the 1 on the left represents 1×2^2. The numeral itself represents the sum $1 \times 2^2 + 0 \times 2^1 + 1 \times 2^0$, which is known as five in the base ten system.

Base Two	Base Ten
$11 = 1 \times 2^1 + 1 \times 2^0$	$= 3$
$1011 = 1 \times 2^3 + 0 \times 2^2 + 1 \times 2^1 + 1 \times 2^0$	$= 11$
$11001 = 1 \times 2^4 + 1 \times 2^3 + 0 \times 2^2 + 0 \times 2^1 + 1 \times 2^0$	$= 25$

To convert a number from base ten to base two we must find which powers of two add up to the number. Since 13 = 8 + 4 + 1, the base two representation for 13 is 1101 (1x8 + 1x4 + 0x2 + 1x1).

Base Ten	Base Two
$6 = 4 + 2 = 1x2^2 + 1x2^1 + 0x2^0$	= 110
$29 = 16 + 8 + 4 + 1 = 1x2^4 + 1x2^3 + 1x2^2 + 0x2^1 + 1x2^0$	= 11101
$52 = 32 + 16 + 4 = 1x2^5 + 1x2^4 + 0x2^3 + 1x2^2 + 0x2^1 + 0x2^0$	= 110100

Computer Memory and Processing

The APPLE is composed of a solid-state electronic memory which stores information and a central processing unit (CPU) which performs calculations, makes decisions, and moves information.

Because electricity has two basic states, ON and OFF, it is ideal for expressing binary numbers. A circuit (called a "flip-flop") when on stands for a "1", and when off stands for a "0". By designing computers to contain millions of simple flip-flop circuits, huge quantities of information can thus be stored.

A single binary digit (0 or 1) is called a "bit", and eight of these bits constitute a "byte". Integers and single characters require one byte of memory for storage. The memory stores both instructions for the CPU and data as binary digits.

The power of a computer is vastly increased when it is capable of storing letters and special characters as well as numbers. In order to do this, a code has been established to translate letters and special characters into numbers which can then be stored in binary form. This code has been standardized by the computer industry as the American Standard Code for Information (ASCII). In this code, each letter of the alphabet, both upper case and lower case, each symbol, and each control function used by the computer is represented by a number. For example, the name JIM is translated by the computer into ASCII numbers 74, 73, 77. In turn these numbers are then stored by the computer in binary form.

J = 74 = 01001010
I = 73 = 01001001
M = 77 = 01001101

In order for the computer to store a name such as JIM, or any piece of non-numeric information, it must be entered in the form of a string, converted character by character into ASCII numbers, and then stored in memory as binary numbers. The following is a table of the ASCII character codes available on the APPLE.

The following is a table of the ASCII character codes.

Decimal Value	ASCII Character	Usage	Decimal Value	ASCII Character	Usage	Decimal Value	ASCII Character	Usage
0	NUL	FILL character	43	+		86	V	
1	SOH		44	,	COMMA	87	W	
2	STX		45	-		88	X	
3	ETX	CTRL/C	46	.		89	Y	
4	EOT		47	/		90	Z	
5	ENQ		48	0		91	[	
6	ACK		49	1		92	/	Back-slash
7	BEL	BELL	50	2		93	]	
8	BS		51	3		94	ˆ or ↑	
9	HT	HORIZ. TAB	52	4		95	— or ←	
10	LF	LINE FEED	53	5		96	`	Grave accent
11	VT		54	6		97	a	
12	FF		55	7		98	b	
13	CR	CAR. RET	56	8		99	c	
14	SO		57	9		100	d	
15	SI	CTRL/O	58	:		101	e	
16	DLE		59	;		102	f	
17	DC1	CTRL/Q	60	<		103	g	
18	DC2		61	&		104	h	
19	DC3	CTRL/S	62	>		105	i	
20	DC4		63	?		106	j	
21	NAK		64	=		107	k	
22	SYN		65	A		108	l	
23	ETB		66	B		109	m	
24	CAN		67	C		110	n	
25	EM		68	D		111	o	
26	SUB		69	E		112	p	
27	ESC	ESCAPE	70	F		113	q	
28	FS		71	G		114	r	
29	GS		72	H		115	s	
30	RS		73	I		116	t	
31	US		74	J		117	u	
32	SP	SPACE	75	K		118	v	
33	!		76	L		119	w	
34	*		77	M		120	x	
35	#		78	N		121	y	
36	$		79	O		122	z	
37	%		80	P		123	{	
38	&		81	Q		124	|	Vertical Line
39	‘	APOSTRO-PHE	82	R		125	}	
40	(		83	S		126	~	Tilde
41	)		84	T		127	DEL RUBOUT	
42	*		85	U				

ASCII Code—ASCII Character Conversions

The conversion of strings into numbers is accomplished by the use of the ASCII code. Commands exist to convert strings into ASCII values and vice versa.

Function format	Operation
X = ASC (P$)	Converts only the first character of the string P$ to its ASCII code number.
M$ = CHR$ (K)	Assigns the character with the ASCII code number of K to the string of M$.

PROGRAM 9.1

This program inputs a character at line 10 and then prints its ASCII code number at line 20. Line 30 prints the character whose ASCII value is two more than that of the input character.

```
10   INPUT "CHARACTER TO BE CONVERTED? ";A$
20   PRINT "THAT'S ASCII CODE "; ASC (A$)
30   PRINT "TWO CHARACTERS AFTER THAT IS "; CHR$ ( ASC (A$) + 2)

]RUN
CHARACTER TO BE CONVERTED? H
THAT'S ASCII CODE 72
TWO CHARACTERS AFTER THAT IS J
```

String Manipulation Functions

Strings can be manipulated using the following functions:

Function	Operation
L$ = LEFT$(A$,N)	Assigns L$ a substring of the string A$ from the leftmost character to and including the Nth character.
L = LEN(A$)	Assigns L a value equal to the number of characters in the string A$, including blank spaces.
M$ = MID$(A$,N)	Assigns M$ a substring of the string A$ from the Nth character to the rightmost character of the string.
M$ = MID$(A$, N1, N2)	Assigns M$ a substring of the string A$, starting with the character N1 and being N2 characters long.
R$ = RIGHT$(A$,N)	Assigns R$ a substring of the string A$ consisting of the rightmost N characters.
S$ = STR$(X)	Converts X into a string of numeric characters and assigns it to S$.
V = VAL(A$)	Converts the first set of numeric characters in the string A$ into a numeric value that is assigned to V. Non-numeric characters are ignored.

PROGRAM 9.2

This program uses string functions to print parts of the string "COMPUTER   ".

```
10 A$ = "COMPUTER  "
20  PRINT  LEFT$ (A$,2)
30  PRINT  RIGHT$ (A$,2)
40  PRINT  MID$ (A$,4)
50  PRINT  MID$ (A$,2,5)
60  PRINT  LEN (A$)

]RUN
CO

PUTER
OMPUT
10
```

PROGRAM 9.3

The following program removes the two left characters from the string "35 HORSES" and then converts them into the number 35 using VAL.

```
10 A$ = "35 HORSES"
20 X =  VAL ( LEFT$ (A$,2))
30  PRINT A$;" HAVE ";4 * X;" LEGS."

]RUN
35 HORSES HAVE 140 LEGS.
```

EXERCISES

PART A

1. Print a table showing the values of x, 2↑x, and 10↑x for x=5 to -5.

2. Input three letters, add their ASCII numbers, find the INT of one third of their sum, and print the character corresponding to the result. Is there any meaning to this process?

3. Using properly selected ASCII numbers on a DATA line, print the sentence "ASCII DID THIS!"

4. Using ASCII numbers 45 and 46 and the PRINT TAB statement, print the following figure.

```
]RUN
.---------.
.         .
.         .
.         .
.---------.
```

5. Enter the string THREE!@#$%STRING!@#$%FUNCTIONS. Use LEFT$, MID$, and RIGHT$ to print the phrase "THREE STRING FUNCTIONS".

6. Enter a string A$ of any length. Print the length of A$ and the ASCII number of its first and last characters.

7. Enter a string A$, and use a loop to print the ASCII number of each of its characters.

8. Let A$="2598". Have the computer apply VAL to those parts of A$ whose sum is 123.

9. Enter the words "QUEEN", "LENGTH", and "REMEMBER". Print each word with all E's removed.

10. Use the computer or a hand calculator to find the binary equivalents of the decimal numerals given below.

    89, 74, 80, 107, 255, 129, 28, 39, 29, 24, 43

11. Use the computer or a hand calculator to find the decimal equivalents for the binary numerals given below.

    1011, 10100, 1111, 1110, 1010011, 110011, 1011100,
    1101111, 11000000, 10000111

12. Input a string A$ which consists of the digits 0 to 9, inclusive, each to be used only once (e.g., 1956472038). Use string functions to obtain from A$ two numbers N1 and N2, N1 being the number represented by the first three digits of A$ and N2 the number represented by the last three digits. Print the sum of N1 and N2.

13. Let A$ consist of the first twelve letters of the alphabet. Using A$, construct the right triangle shown at the right.

```
]RUN
A
AB
ABC
ABCD
ABCDE
ABCDEF
ABCDEFG
ABCDEFGH
ABCDEFGHI
ABCDEFGHIJ
ABCDEFGHIJK
ABCDEFGHIJKL
```

14. As a young boy Franklin Roosevelt signed his letters to his mother backwards: TLEVESOOR NILKNARF. Write a program that accepts a person's name and prints it backwards.

15. Using the ASCII chart given in the text, determine the output for the following program. Check by running the program.

```
10  FOR A = 1 TO 4
20  READ A$
30  PRINT  ASC (A$),
40  NEXT A
50  DATA  "W","H","7","625"
```

16. The output of the following program is Foxy Moxie's message to Jimmy Band. What is the message? Check by running the program.

```
10  FOR W = 1 TO 6
20  READ A$,B$,C$
30  PRINT  LEFT$ (A$,1); MID$ (B$,2,2); RIGHT$ (C$,1)
40  NEXT W
50  DATA  FGT,LOXK,NTY
60  DATA  SFJ,DAYT,GES
70  DATA  HWT,QELM,BIP
80  DATA  WJG,WILS,WZL
90  DATA  CDE,HOMV,PSE
100  DATA  SOA,AOOC,TZN
```

17. Choose fifteen random integers from 65 to 90, inclusive, to serve as ASCII code numbers. Convert these fifteen integers to the fifteen characters for which they stand, and print the results.

18. Write a program which produces a sentence containing twenty nonsense words. Each word can contain from two to five letters. Use random numbers and the ASCII code to produce the words.

```
]RUN
SQIF XXDP MV TFJI QJ IOP XERT CJI LVIL MMPSD MOP QAJU HK VIRI
FDS IKQU KIKI MULSA MMGY BLOT
```

19. Using random numbers and the ASCII code numbers from 32 to 126, inclusive, have the computer generate a string of 100 characters, allowing repetitions. Tabulate how many characters are letters, numbers, or miscellaneous characters. Print the results.

20. Using string functions, write a program to play a word guessing game. Ask the player to guess a secret word. Search through each guess to see if the guess contains any correct letters. If any letter is correct, have the computer print the ones that are. If the entire word is guessed, type "YOU GUESSED IT!!"

```
]RUN
GUESS A WORD? SUE
GUESS A WORD? HARRIET
H IS IN THE WORD
A IS IN THE WORD
GUESS A WORD? BASEBALL
A IS IN THE WORD
A IS IN THE WORD
GUESS A WORD? GRUMP
G IS IN THE WORD
M IS IN THE WORD
GUESS A WORD? HANGMAN
YOU GUESSED IT!!
```

21. You are a spy who will use the computer to produce a secret code.

(A) Input a short message, and have the computer type back what appears to be nonsense words. To produce the coded words, convert each letter of the original message into its corresponding ASCII code number, add two to each number, and convert to characters to produce the message. Keep all spaces between the words in their original places, and understand that the letters Y and Z are to be converted to A and B.

(B) Write a program that will decode the message.

22. When the following program is run the output is:

A = 1500   B = 999.999908

Explain in a clear, brief manner why the value of B is not exactly 1000, and why the value of A is exactly 1500.

```
10  FOR X = 1 TO 3000
20 A = A + 1 / 2:B = B + 1 / 3
30  NEXT X
40  PRINT "A = ";A,"B = ";B
```

23. Often, literary critics argue over the true identity of the author of some ancient manuscript. To resolve such disputes, it is helpful to show similarities between the anonymous text and a text by a known author. Write a program which tabulates the occurrences of each article ("a", "an", and "the"), each adverb (check for "ly"), and of each mark of punctuation (".", "!", "?", ";",":").

24. Create bizarre "sentences" by having the computer print the words of a real sentence in reverse order. Your program should NOT reverse the order of the letters in each word.

25. Last night you were informed that your aunt had left you several million dollars. You decide to start your own corporation. In the tradition of DEC, GTE, RCA, WE, and other great corporate conglomerates, you want your corporate name to be composed of as many initials as you like, each standing for a word (e.g., Radio Corporation of America becomes RCA). Write a program which accepts up to ten words and then prints a block of letters composed of the first letters of each word. For example, given "WE AWAIT SILENT TRYSTERO'S EMPIRE", the program should return "WASTE".

26. Write a program which prints a triangle made up of parts of the word "triangle". The triangle should be obtuse, and the program should ask for its height, how far to indent the bottom edge, and where the bottom edge ends.

```
T
 RI
  IAN
   ANGL
    NGLET
     GLETRI
      LETRIAN
       ETRIANGL
        TRIANGLET
          IANGLETRIA
           ANGLETRIANG
            NGLETRIANGLE
             GLETRIANGLETR
              LETRIANGLETRIA
               ETRIANGLETRIANG
                TRIANGLETRIANGLE
                 RIANGLETRIANGLETR
                  IANGLETRIANGLETRIA
```

27. Enter a positive integer N$ as it would be expressed in binary form. That is, enter a string of ones and zeroes. Have the computer print the equivalent of N$ as it is expressed in the decimal system. One method is to use synthetic substitution.

APPENDIX A

Starting Programs in the Middle

Entering a line number after a RUN command will cause the APPLE to start running the program in memory at the specified line instead of at the beginning.

```
10  PRINT "AT 10"
20  PRINT "AT 20"

]RUN
AT 10
AT 20

]RUN 20
AT 20

]
```

STOP

When the computer encounters a STOP command, it will immediately halt execution of the program.

```
10  PRINT "AT 10"
20  STOP
30  PRINT "AT 30"

]RUN
AT 10

BREAK IN 20
]
```

CONT

Execution of a halted program can be resumed by typing CONT only if the halt was caused by a STOP or a CTRL-C. The program will restart at the point where it stopped but only if no errors occurred in the immediate mode while the program was stopped and no changes were made in the program.

```
10   FOR X = 1 TO 10
20   PRINT X
30   NEXT X

]RUN
1
2
3
4
5

BREAK IN 20
]CONT
6
7
8
9
10

]
```

GET

The GET command is used in place of INPUT to take a single digit or character from the keyboard without having to press the RETURN key. The digit or character is not printed on the screen as the key is struck.

```
10   GET A$
20   IF A$ = "-" THEN 50
30 B$ = B$ + A$
40   GOTO 10
50   PRINT "B$ = ";B$

]RUN
B$ = MARY HAD A LITTLE LAMB

]
```

FRE

PRINT FRE(0)

will return the number of free bytes left in memory available to the user. If there are more than 32767 bytes available, FRE(0) will return a negative number. To obtain the proper number, add 65536 to the negative number returned.

```
]PRINT FRE(0)
-29285

]PRINT FRE(0)+65536
36251
```

CLEAR

CLEAR will set all numerical variables to 0 and all string variables to "" while a program is running.

```
10 A = 5:B$ = "(&%(%"
20  PRINT A,B$
30  CLEAR
40  PRINT A,B$

]RUN
5               (&%(%
0

]
```

CTRL-X

Typing the CTRL and X keys at the same time tells the APPLE to ignore the line currently being typed. A backslash (\) appears and the cursor moves to the next line.

```
]10 FOR X=1 TO 5

]20 PRINT X+8

]20 NEXT X\
]30 NEXT X

]RUN
9
10
11
12
13

]
```

ESC A, B, C or D

The escape key can be used to move the cursor around without affecting anything that is on the screen. Pressing and releasing the ESC key and then pressing the A key will move the cursor one space to the right. Pressing the ESC key and then B will move the cursor to the left. ESC and C will move the cursor down and ESC and D will move it up.

POS

$$A = POS(0)$$

will set A equal to the horizontal position of the cursor on the screen, 0 being the left edge and 39 the right edge.

Using a Tape Recorder

A tape recorder can be connected to the jacks at the back of the APPLE if a disk drive is not used. The CASSETTE IN jack is connected to the EAR jack on the tape recorder and the CASSETTE OUT to the MIC jack. This will allow programs and data to be saved and then recalled at a later date.

Saving a Program, SAVE

After entering your program in the computer, start the tape recorder in record mode, and type SAVE. The APPLE will beep to indicate that it has started to write on the tape. When the program has been stored, the computer beeps again, and the tape recorder can be turned off.

Recalling a Program, LOAD

Rewind the tape so that it is at the beginning of the section in which your program is stored. Start the tape recorder in playback mode, and type LOAD. The computer beeps once when it starts to recall the program and again when it is finished. The program is then ready to run, and the tape recorder can be turned off.

Storing Data, STORE

The APPLE can store data on tape in the form of numeric subscripted variables. Once a subscripted variable has been dimensioned and the individual elements have been assigned their values, the command STORE will record the information on tape.

```
10  DIM A(15)
20  FOR B = 1 TO 15
30 A(B) = B ^ 2
40  NEXT B
50  INPUT "TURN ON THE TAPE, THEN HIT RETURN;"Z$
60  STORE A
```

Note that line 60 stores all 15 elements of the subscripted variable A.

Recalling Data, RECALL

The values of a numeric subscripted variable which has been previously stored on tape can be retrieved by using the RECALL command. The tape recorder must be in playback mode, and the program must contain an appropriate DIM statement.

```
10   DIM A(15)
20   INPUT "TURN ON THE TAPE, THEN HIT RETURN";Z$
30   RECALL A
40   FOR Q = 1 TO 15
50   PRINT A(Q);"   ";
60   NEXT Q
```

It is important that the recalled subscripted variable be dimensioned exactly as the stored subscripted variable. Otherwise, the data will not be read properly.

Keeping Strings on Tape

STORE and RECALL cannot be used with strings directly. In using the ASC function, strings must be converted to numeric data which is then stored in a numeric subscripted variable. The following two programs will store and retrieve a string up to 255 characters long.

```
10   INPUT A$
20   DIM A(255)
30   FOR Q = 1 TO  LEN (A$)
40 A(Q) =  ASC ( MID$ (A$,Q,1))
50   NEXT Q
60 A(0) =  LEN (A$)
70   INPUT "TURN ON THE TAPE, THEN HIT RETURN";Z$
80   STORE A
```

```
10   DIM A(255)
20   INPUT "TURN ON THE TAPE, THEN HIT RETURN";Z$
30   RECALL A
40   FOR W = 1 TO A(0)
50 A$ = A$ +  CHR$ (A(W))
60   NEXT W
70   PRINT A$
```

Note that A(0) is used to store the length of A$. Further explanation of ASC, CHR$ and LEN can be found in Chapter 9.

PEEK and POKE

PEEK is used to retrieve the contents of the APPLE's memory. For example,

```
]PRINT PEEK(500)
0
```

will print the contents of memory at location 500. In this case it was 0.

POKE is used to insert something into the APPLE's memory. For example,

```
POKE 250,42
```

will put a 42 in location 250 of memory.

Except as stated in the other parts of the book, PEEK and POKE should be used only by very experienced programmers. Incorrect use of PEEK and POKE can drastically impair the proper operation of the APPLE.

APPENDIX B

DOS INSTRUCTIONS

Proper Use of Equipment

Strong magnetic fields, heat, or bending affect the operation of diskettes. Therefore they must not be placed near devices which produce magnetic fields or heat (e.g., television sets). When being loaded, the diskette should be slid gently into the disk drive, never forced.

The disk drive will run endlessly, possibly damaging it, if it is run either without a diskette or with an uninitialized diskette. Pressing the RESET key will stop it.

Making a Disk Operational, INIT

To insert a diskette, flip up the cover of the drive, and carefully slide the diskette in with its label up. The diskette should be grasped by the right hand with the thumb on the label and the forefinger underneath.

In the case of the APPLE II PLUS, the diskette becomes operational automatically when the unit is turned on. To make the earlier APPLE II recognize the disk, type PR#n, where n is the number of the slot in which the disk controller card is installed.

New Diskettes

A new diskette must be initialized before it can be used. First, type NEW, and write a program which will identify the diskette. The following example is given.

```
10   REM  I.D. PROGRAM
20   PRINT "DISKETTE #3"
30   PRINT "INITIALIZED BY"
40   PRINT "SANDRA COOK"
50   PRINT "10/26/81"
60   PRINT
```

When the program has been entered, type INIT HELLO. This initializes the diskette, with the identifying program being named HELLO (other names are acceptable). Each time the computer is turned on with this disk in Drive 1, the identifying program will run automatically.

MAXFILES

Normally the APPLE can have up to three files open simultaneously. To increase this limit, type MAXFILES n in immediate mode, where n is the number of files to be open at one time. The larger n is made, however, the less space will be available in the computer's memory for your program. Each open file takes up 256 bytes of memory for a buffer. For example,

```
MAXFILES 5
```

SAVE

To save a program on a disk, type SAVE followed by the name to be used to identify the program on the disk. For example,

```
SAVE JONES
```

DELETE

To remove a program or file from a diskette, type DELETE, either in a program or immediate mode, followed by the name of the program or file. For example,

```
DELETE JONES
```

or

```
80 PRINT CHR$(4); "DELETE JONES"
```

RENAME

To change the name of a program or file, type RENAME, either in a program or immediate mode, followed by the old name, a comma, and the new name. For example,

```
RENAME SMITH, JONES
```

or

```
80 PRINT CHR$(4); "RENAME SMITH, JONES"
```

CATALOG

Typing CATALOG, either in a program or immediate mode, produces a list of all programs and files on a diskette. For example,

```
CATALOG
```

or

```
80 PRINT CHR$(4); "CATALOG"
```

REVIEW ANSWERS

CHAPTER ONE

1.
```
10 X = 5
20 Y = 5 * X + 7
30  PRINT Y
```

2.
```
10 A$ = "HARRY"
20 B$ = "JUDY"
30  PRINT "HELLO ";A$
40  PRINT "HOW ARE YOU?"
50  PRINT B$;" IS LOOKING FOR YOU."
```

3.
```
10  READ X
20 Y = 3 * X + 5
30  PRINT Y
40  GOTO 10
50  DATA  3,5,12,17,8
```

4.
```
10  PRINT "NAME","FIRST GRADE"
20  READ N$,A,B,C,D
30  PRINT N$,A
40  GOTO 20
50  DATA  WATERS,83,75,52,80, PARTRIDGE,74,81,92,76,
HAYDEN,72,81,63,60
```

5.
```
10  INPUT X
20  PRINT "5*X= ";5 * X
30  PRINT "X/5= ";X / 5
40  GOTO 10
```

6.
```
10  INPUT "WHAT IS YOUR NAME? ";N$
20  INPUT "WHAT IS YOUR FRIEND'S NAME? ";A$
30  PRINT A$;" IS A FRIEND OF ";N$
40  PRINT
50  GOTO 10
```

CHAPTER TWO

1.
```
10  INPUT "ENTER TWO NUMBERS? ";A,B
20  IF A > B THEN  PRINT A,B: GOTO 10
30  PRINT B,A: GOTO 10
```

2.
```
10  INPUT "ENTER TWO LAST NAMES? ";A$,B$
20  IF A$ < B$ THEN  PRINT A$: PRINT B$: GOTO 10
30  PRINT B$: PRINT A$: GOTO 10
```

3.
```
10  INPUT "ENTER A NUMBER? ";N
20  IF N > 25 AND N < 112 THEN 40
30  PRINT N;" IS OUT OF RANGE": GOTO 10
40  PRINT N;" IS BETWEEN 25 AND 112": GOTO 10
```

4.
```
10  INPUT A$,B$,C$: PRINT A$;B$;C$
```

5.
```
10  FOR X = 1 TO 25
20  PRINT " ";X;
30  NEXT X
```

6.
```
10  FOR A = 10 TO 1 STEP  - 1
20  PRINT A;" ";
30  NEXT A
```

7.
```
10  INPUT "STEP VALUE? ";N
20  FOR T = 8 TO 20 STEP N
30  PRINT T;" ";
40  NEXT T
```

CHAPTER THREE

1.
```
10  FOR X = 1 TO 12
20 R =  INT (26 *  RND (1) + 250)
30  PRINT R;" ";
40  NEXT X
```

2.
```
10 R =  INT (50 *  RND (1) + 1)
20  FOR X = 1 TO 5
30  INPUT "WHAT IS YOUR GUESS? ";G
40  IF G = R THEN 120
50  IF G < R THEN 70
60  PRINT "TOO HIGH": GOTO 80
70  PRINT "TOO LOW"
80  NEXT X
90  PRINT "YOU HAVE MADE TOO MANY MISTAKES."
100  PRINT "THE NUMBER WAS ";R
110  END
120  PRINT "YOU ARE CORRECT!"
```

3.
```
10  FOR X = 1 TO 50
20 R =  INT (10 *  RND (1))
30  IF R < 5 THEN A = A + 1: GOTO 50
40 B = B + 1
50  NEXT X
60  PRINT "(0-4): ";A
70  PRINT "(5-9): ";B
```

4.
```
10  FOR X = 1 TO 10
20  INPUT A
30  IF A / 2 =  INT (A / 2) THEN E = E + 1: GOTO 50
40 O = O + 1
50  NEXT X
60  PRINT
70  PRINT E;" EVEN",O;" ODD"
```

CHAPTER FOUR

1.
```
10  FOR X = 21 TO 24
20  PRINT "X=";X
30  FOR Y = 1 TO 3
40  PRINT "Y=";Y
50  NEXT Y: NEXT X
```

2.

```
10   FOR X = 1 TO 3
20   INPUT A(X)
30   NEXT X
40   PRINT
50   FOR X = 3 TO 1 STEP  - 1
60   PRINT A(X)
70   NEXT X
```

3.

```
10   FOR X = 1 TO 6
20   INPUT W$(X)
30   NEXT X
40   FOR Y = 1 TO 4
50   PRINT W$( INT ( RND (1) * 6 + 1));" ";
60   NEXT Y
70   PRINT "."
```

4.

```
10   FOR X = 1 TO 6
20   INPUT W$(X)
30   NEXT X
40   FOR Y = 1 TO 4
50 A =  INT ( RND (1) * 6 + 1)
60   IF W$(A) = "" THEN 50
70   PRINT W$(A);" ";
80 W$(A) = ""
90   NEXT Y
```

5.

```
5   DIM X(6)
10   FOR I = 1 TO 6
20   INPUT X(I)
30   NEXT I
40   FOR I = 1 TO 6
50   PRINT X(I)
60   NEXT I
70   PRINT
80   FOR I = 1 TO 6
90   PRINT X(I);" ";
100  NEXT I
```

6.

```
10   DIM X$(5,3)
20   FOR I = 1 TO 5
30   FOR J = 1 TO 3
40   READ X$(I,J)
50   NEXT J: NEXT I
60   FOR J = 1 TO 3
70   FOR I = 1 TO 5
80   PRINT X$(I,J);" ";
90   NEXT I: PRINT : NEXT J
100  DATA  A,B,C,D,E,F,G,H,I,J,K,L,M,N,O
```

CHAPTER SIX

1.
```
10  GR
20  COLOR= 12
30  HLIN 0,39 AT 0: HLIN 0,39 AT 39
40  VLIN 1,38 AT 0: VLIN 1,38 AT 39
50  REM  LINE 30 DRAWS TOP & BOTTOM LINES
60  REM  LINE 40 DRAWS THE SIDE LINES
```

2.
```
10  GR
20  REM  PLOT THE RED BACKGROUND
30  COLOR= 1
40  FOR Y = 0 TO 39
50  HLIN 0,39 AT Y
60  NEXT Y
70  REM  PLOT THE BLUE POINT
80  COLOR= 6
90  PLOT 19,19
```

3.
```
10  GR
20  FOR X = 1 TO 15: COLOR= X
30  VLIN 0,39 AT X
40  NEXT X: END
```

4.
```
10  HGR
20  INPUT "X,Y? ";X,Y
30 C =  INT ( RND (1) * 8)
40  PRINT "HCOLOR = ";C
50  HCOLOR= C
60  HPLOT X,Y
70  GOTO 20
```

5.
```
10  HGR
20  FOR C = 1 TO 7
30  HCOLOR= C
40  HPLOT 0,C * 10 TO 279,C * 10
50  NEXT C
```

6.

```
10  HGR2 : HCOLOR= 5
20 X0 = 115:Y0 = 150
30  REM  DRAW AXES
40  HPLOT 0,Y0 TO 279,Y0
50  HPLOT X0,0 TO X0,191
60  REM  GRAPH FUNCTION
70  FOR X1 = 0 TO 279
80 X = X1 - X0
90 Y = (1 / 5) * X ^ 2 - 8
100 Y1 = Y0 - Y
110  IF (Y1 >  = 0) AND (Y1 <  = 191) THEN  HPLOT X1,Y1
120  NEXT X1
```

EXERCISE ANSWERS

CHAPTER ONE

1.
```
10   PRINT "A"
20   PRINT " B"
30   PRINT "  C"
40   PRINT "ABCD"
```

3.
```
]RUN
THE VALUE OF B
19
```

5.
```
10   READ A,B
20   PRINT "THE SUM IS ";A + B
30   GOTO 10
40   DATA  12,8,9,5
```

7.
```
10   INPUT "PRICE, NUMBER OF LOAVES? ";P,N
20   PRINT "TOTAL SPENT = $";P * N / 100
```

9.
```
10   INPUT X,Y
20   PRINT "X=";X,"Y=";Y,"X*Y=";X * Y
30   GOTO 10
```

11.
```
]RUN
300               510
.3   .51
```

13.
```
]PRINT "  AAA";111,222;"AAA","333";"  ";16-3*2
 AAA111          222AAA            333   10
```

15.
```
]RUN
ABCDXYZ
ABCD7
7XYZ
-4XYZ
```

17.
```
10  PRINT 2 + 3 + 4 + 3 + 5
```

19.
```
10  READ X,Y
20 A = 12 * X + 7 * Y
30  PRINT A
40  GOTO 10
50  DATA  3,2,7,9,12,-4
```

21.
```
10  INPUT "LENGTH, WIDTH, AND HEIGHT? ";L,W,H
20  PRINT "VOLUME IS ";L * W * H
```

23.
```
10  INPUT "HEIGHT? ";H
20  INPUT "WIDTH? ";W
30  INPUT "LENGTH? ";L
40  INPUT "PRESENCE? ";P
50  PRINT "YOUR OBJECT TAKES UP ";H * W * L * P;" TESSERACTS IN FOUR-SPACE
60  GOTO 10
```

25.
```
10  INPUT "HOW MANY BOOKS HAVE YOU BORROWED? ";B
20  INPUT "HOW MANY DAYS LATE ARE THEY? ";L
30  PRINT "YOU OWE ";.10 * B * L;" DOLLARS."
```

27.
```
10  INPUT "WHAT IS THE PLAYER'S NAME? ";P$
20  PRINT "WHAT IS ";P$;"'S ";
30  INPUT "WAGE? ";W
40 T = W * .44
50  PRINT P$;" WOULD KEEP $";W - T
60  PRINT "HE WOULD PAY $";T;" IN TAXES."
```

29.
```
10  INPUT "WHAT IS THE BASE? ";B
20  INPUT "WHAT IS THE ALTITUDE? ";A
30 T = A * B * .5
40  PRINT
50  PRINT "THE AREA IS ";T
```

31.
```
10 READ S1,G1,S2,G2,S3,G3,S4,G4,S5,G5
20 S = S1 + S2 + S3 + S4 + S5
30 G = G1 + G2 + G3 + G4 + G5
40 T = S + G
50 PRINT "SLOTH'S TOTAL VOTE WAS ";S
60 PRINT "HIS PERCENTAGE WAS ";100 * S / T
70 PRINT
80 PRINT "GRAFT'S TOTAL VOTE WAS ";G
90 PRINT "HIS PERCENTAGE WAS ";100 * G / T
100 DATA 528,210,313,721,1003,822,413,1107,516,1700
```

33.
```
10 INPUT "MONTH, DAY, AND YEAR OF BIRTH? ";M1,D1,Y1
20 D9 = Y1 * 365 + M1 * 30 + D1
30 INPUT "TODAY'S MONTH, DAY, AND YEAR? ";M2,D2,Y2
40 D8 = Y2 * 365 + M2 * 30 + D2
50 S = 8 * (D8 - D9)
60 PRINT "YOU HAVE SLEPT ABOUT ";S;" HOURS."
```

CHAPTER TWO

1.
```
10 INPUT A,B
20 IF A < B THEN 60
30 IF A > B THEN 80
40 PRINT A;" IS EQUAL TO ";B
50 GOTO 10
60 PRINT A;" IS LESS THAN ";B
70 GOTO 10
80 PRINT A;" IS GREATER THAN ";B
90 GOTO 10
```

3.
```
10 INPUT A$
20 IF A$ > "MIDWAY" THEN  PRINT A$
```

5.
```
10 INPUT A$,B$: PRINT A$,B$: PRINT B$,A$
```

7.
```
10 INPUT A$
20 IF A$ > "DOWN" AND A$ < "UP" THEN  PRINT "A$ IS BETWEEN"
```

9.
```
10 INPUT X
20 IF X <  = 25 OR X >  = 75 THEN 50
30 PRINT "IN THE INTERVAL"
40 GOTO 10
50 PRINT "NOT IN THE INTERVAL"
60 GOTO 10
```

11.
```
10  FOR X = 11 TO  - 11 STEP  - 2
20  PRINT X ^ 3,
30  NEXT X
```

13.
```
10  FOR Q = 1 TO 40
20  PRINT "*";
30  NEXT Q: PRINT
```

15.
```
10  FOR X = 10 TO 97 STEP 3
20  PRINT X,
30  NEXT X
```

17.
```
10  INPUT "CREATURE? ";X$
20  RESTORE
30  FOR N = 1 TO 6: READ C$,W$
40  IF C$ = X$ THEN 80
50  NEXT N
60  PRINT "CREATURE ";X$;" NOT FOUND."
70  GOTO 10
80  PRINT "YOU CAN KILL A ";C$;" WITH A ";W$
90  GOTO 10
100  DATA LICH,"FIRE BALL",MUMMY,"FLAMING TORCH"
110  DATA  WEREWOLF,"SILVER BULLET",VAMPIRE,"WOODEN STAKE"
120  DATA MEDUSA,"SHARP SWORD",TRIFFID,"FIRE HOSE"
```

19. **LINE: #10 #20 #30 #40 #50 #60 #10**
#20 #30 #40 #50 #60 #10 #20 #30 #40 END

21.
```
10  FOR R = 1 TO 10
20  PRINT : PRINT "-----------------------"
30  PRINT "  HAPPY HOLIDAY MOTEL"
40  PRINT "          ROOM ";R
50  PRINT "-----------------------"
60  NEXT R
```

23.
```
10  PRINT "X","X^2","X^3": PRINT
20  FOR X = 2 TO 10 STEP 2
30  PRINT X,X ^ 2,X ^ 3
40  NEXT X
```

25.
```
10  INPUT N
20  FOR H = 1 TO N
30  IF W = H THEN 70
40  PRINT "*";
50 W = W + 1
60  GOTO 30
70  PRINT :W = 0
80  NEXT H
90  END
```

27.
```
10   FOR L = 1 TO 5
20   READ N$,P
30   IF P > = 75 THEN 100
40   PRINT : PRINT "DEAR ";N$;","
50   PRINT "  I AM SO SORRY THAT I MUST FIRE YOU."
60   PRINT "YOU HAVE BEEN SUCH A FINE EMPLOYEE"
70   PRINT "WITH A PERFORMANCE RATING OF ";P;"%"
80   PRINT "I'M SURE YOU'LL HAVE NO TROUBLE"
90   PRINT "FINDING ANOTHER JOB.": PRINT  TAB( 20);"SINCERELY,"
95   PRINT : PRINT  TAB( 20);"GEORGE SHWABB": PRINT
100  NEXT L
110  DATA  OAKLEY,69,HOWE,92,ANDERSON,96,WOLLEY,88,GOERZ,74
```

CHAPTER THREE

1.
```
10  FOR I = 1 TO 10
20 X =  RND (1)
30  IF X > .5 THEN  PRINT X
40  NEXT I
```

3.
```
10  INPUT N
20  IF N <  >  INT (N) THEN 10
30  PRINT N
```

5.
```
10 N =  INT (4 *  RND (1) + 2)
20 D =  INT (4 *  RND (1) + 1)
30 Q =  INT (4 *  RND (1))
40 C = 5 * N + 10 * D + 25 * Q
50  IF C >  = 99 THEN  PRINT "YOU GET LUNCH.": GOTO 70
60  PRINT "NO LUNCH!"
70  PRINT C;" CENTS FOUND."
```

7.
```
10 T = 11
20  FOR W = 1 TO 4
30  INPUT "NUMBER ADDED? ";N
40 T = T + N
50  PRINT "VALUE = $";T / 100
60  NEXT W
```

9.
```
10  HOME
20  FOR X = 1 TO 24
30  HTAB (X): VTAB (X)
40  PRINT "*"
50  NEXT X
```

11A.
```
]RUN
1
 2
  3
   4
                1
                2
                3
                4
```

11B.
```
]RUN
123.4           123.5
123.45          123.46
```

13.
```
X               Y
-               -
1*              5*
2               0
                2
                1
                -1
3*              2*

* - THIS SHOULD BE CIRCLED.
```

15.
```
10  FOR N = 13 TO 147 STEP 2
20 S = S + N
30  NEXT N
40  PRINT "THE SUM = ";S
```

17.
```
10  FOR X = 1 TO 1000
20 N =  INT (9 *  RND (1) + 1)
30  IF N / 2 =  INT (N / 2) THEN E = E + 1: GOTO 50
40 D = D + 1
50  NEXT X
60  PRINT "THERE WERE ";D;" ODD INTEGERS."
70  PRINT "THERE WERE ";E;" EVEN INTEGERS."
```

19.
```
10 Y = 1980:B = 1000
20  PRINT "DATE","BALANCE"
30 Y = Y + 1:B = B +  INT (5 * B) / 100
40  PRINT "JAN 1, ";Y,"$";B
50  IF B < 2000 THEN 30
```

21.
```
10  READ V
20 R = ((V * .75) / 3.14159) ^ 1 / 3
30  PRINT V, INT (R * 100 + .5) / 100
40  GOTO 10
50  DATA  690,720,460,620
```

23.
```
10   PRINT  TAB( 15);"*"
20   FOR X = 1 TO 5
30   PRINT  TAB( 15 - X);"*"; TAB( 15 + X);"*"
40   NEXT X
50   PRINT  TAB( 9);"*************"
```

25.
```
5  HOME
10 R = 5:X = 20:Y = 12
20  FOR Y1 =  - 5 TO 5
30 X1 =  SQR (R ^ 2 - Y1 ^ 2)
40  HTAB ( INT (X + X1 + .5)): VTAB ( INT (Y + Y1 + .5))
50  PRINT "*";
60  HTAB ( INT (X - X1 + .5)): VTAB ( INT (Y + Y1 + .5))
70  PRINT "*";
90  NEXT Y1
```

27.
```
10 Q =  INT (8 *  RND (1))
20 D =  INT (5 *  RND (1))
30 P =  INT (10 *  RND (1))
40 C = Q + D + P:V = .25 * Q + .1 * D + .01 * P
50  PRINT "THERE ARE ";C;" COINS."
60  PRINT "WORTH $";V
70  FOR X = 1 TO 10
80  INPUT "QUARTERS? ";Q1
90  INPUT "DIMES? ";D1
100  INPUT "PENNIES? ";P1
110  IF Q = Q1 AND D = D1 AND P = P1 THEN 170
120  PRINT "WRONG": PRINT
130  NEXT X
140  PRINT "THERE WERE ";Q;" QUARTER(S), ";D;" DIME(S) AND "
150  PRINT P;" PENNIE(S)."
160  END
170  FLASH : PRINT "CORRECT": NORMAL
```

29.
```
10 X1 =  INT (40 *  RND (1) + 1):Y1 =  INT (24 *  RND (1) + 1)
20 X2 =  INT (40 *  RND (1) + 1):Y2 =  INT (24 *  RND (1) + 1)
30  HOME : HTAB (X1): VTAB (Y1): PRINT "*";
40  HTAB (X2): VTAB (Y2): PRINT "*";
50  FOR Z = 1 TO 10
60  HTAB (1): VTAB (22)
70  INPUT "COORDINATES (X,Y)? ";X,Y
80  IF X = X1 AND Y = Y1 THEN T = T + 1: GOTO 130
90  IF X = X2 AND Y = Y2 THEN T = T + 1: GOTO 150
100  PRINT "MISSED "
110  IF T = 2 THEN 170
120  NEXT Z: GOTO 190
130  PRINT "GOT IT!": HTAB (X1): VTAB (Y1)
140  PRINT " ";: GOTO 110
150  PRINT "GOT IT!": HTAB (X2): VTAB (Y2)
160  PRINT " ";: GOTO 110
170  FLASH : PRINT "YOU HAVE DEFEATED THE EMPIRE!": NORMAL
180  END
190  HOME : VTAB (10): HTAB (5)
200  PRINT "THE EMPIRE HAS WON YOU ";
210  FLASH : PRINT "TURKEY": NORMAL
```

CHAPTER FOUR

1.
```
10  FOR X = 1 TO 8
20  FOR Y = 1 TO 30
30  PRINT "*";
40  NEXT Y
50  PRINT
60  NEXT X
```

3.
```
10  FOR I = 1 TO 6
20  INPUT X(I)
30  NEXT I
40  FOR I = 1 TO 5 STEP 2
50  PRINT I;" ";X(I),
60  NEXT I
70  FOR I = 2 TO 6 STEP 2
80  PRINT I;" ";X(I),
90  NEXT I
```

5.
```
10   DIM A(4,12)
20   FOR I = 1 TO 4
30   FOR J = 1 TO 12
40 A(I,J) = 3 * I + J * J
50   NEXT J
60   NEXT I
70   INPUT N
80   FOR Z = 1 TO 12
90   PRINT A(N,Z);" ";
100   NEXT Z
110   PRINT
120   GOTO 70
```

7A.
```
]RUN
1                    5
1                    6
2                    5
2                    6
3                    5
3                    6
```

7B.
```
]RUN
10
10
10
12
12
11
14
13
11
```

7C.
```
]RUN
45                  89                  35
```

9.
```
10   FOR X = 40 TO 1 STEP  - 1
20   FOR Y = 1 TO 10
30   READ N
40   IF N = X THEN  PRINT N;"   ";
50   NEXT Y
60   RESTORE
70   NEXT X
80   DATA  5,27,37,16,27,8,2,40,1,9
```

11.
```
10   DIM N(100)
20   FOR X = 1 TO 100
30 N(X) =  INT (99 *  RND (1) + 1)
40   FOR Y = 0 TO X - 1
50   IF N(X) = N(Y) THEN 90
60   NEXT Y
70   NEXT X
80   END
90   PRINT "DUPLICATE AFTER ";X;" NUMBERS"
100   FOR Z = 1 TO X
110   PRINT N(Z);" ";
120   NEXT Z
```

Note: Line 40 reads FOR Y=0 TO X-1 so that the new number is not checked against itself.

13.
```
10   FOR X = 1 TO 10
20   FOR Y = X + 1 TO 10
30   FOR Z = Y + 1 TO 10
40   IF X + Y + Z = 16 THEN  PRINT X;" ";Y;" ";Z
50   NEXT Z: NEXT Y: NEXT X
```

15.
```
10   DIM N(20)
20   FOR X = 1 TO 20
30 N(X) =  INT (90 *  RND (1) + 10)
40   NEXT X
50   PRINT "ODD INTEGERS: ";
60   FOR X = 1 TO 20
70   IF N(X) / 2 =  INT (N(X) / 2) THEN 90
80   PRINT N(X);", ";
90   NEXT X: PRINT
100   PRINT "EVEN INTEGERS: ";
110   FOR X = 1 TO 20
120   IF N(X) / 2 < >  INT (N(X) / 2) THEN 140
130   PRINT N(X);", ";
140   NEXT X
```

17A.
```
10   DIM N$(5,6)
20   INPUT "WHAT DAY AND TIME WOULD YOU LIKE? ";D,T
30   IF N$(D,T) < > "" THEN  PRINT "THAT TIME IS TAKEN.": GOTO 20
40   INPUT "WHAT IS YOUR NAME? ";N$(D,T)
50   PRINT "THANK YOU."
60   GOTO 20
```

17B.

```
10   DIM N$(5,6)
15   INPUT "ARE YOU THE DOCTOR? ";A$
17   IF A$ = "YES" THEN 70
20   INPUT "WHAT DAY AND TIME WOULD YOU LIKE? ";D,T
30   IF N$(D,T) <  > "" THEN  PRINT "THAT TIME IS TAKEN.": GOTO 20
40   INPUT "WHAT IS YOUR NAME? ";N$(D,T)
50   PRINT "THANK YOU."
60   GOTO 15
70   INPUT "WHICH DAY? ";D
80   FOR T = 1 TO 6
90   IF N$(D,T) = "" THEN  PRINT "SANKA BREAK": GOTO 110
100   PRINT N$(D,T)
110   NEXT T
120   GOTO 15
```

19.

```
10   DIM N(100)
20 R =  INT (100 *  RND (1) + 1)
30   FOR X = 1 TO 100
40   INPUT "GUESS? ";G
50   IF G = R THEN 150
60   FOR Z = 0 TO X - 1
70   IF N(Z) = G THEN 130
80   NEXT Z
90 N(X) = G
100   IF G > R THEN  PRINT "LOWER": GOTO 120
110   PRINT "HIGHER"
120   NEXT X
130   PRINT "WAKE UP! YOU GUESSED THAT NUMBER BEFORE."
140   GOTO 40
150   PRINT "CORRECT"
```

21.

```
10   DIM P(6,6),B(6,6)
20   FOR E = 1 TO 6
30 P(1,E) = 1:P(6,E) = 1:P(E,1) = 1:P(E,6) = 1
40   NEXT E
50   FOR E = 2 TO 5
60 P(2,E) = 2:P(5,E) = 2:P(E,2) = 2:P(E,5) = 2
70   NEXT E
80   FOR E = 3 TO 4
90 P(3,E) = 3:P(4,E) = 3:P(E,3) = 3:P(E,4) = 3
100   NEXT E
110   FOR Q = 1 TO 6: FOR W = 1 TO 6
120 B(Q,W) = P(Q,W)
130   NEXT W: NEXT Q
140   FOR L = 1 TO 10
150 R =  INT (6 *  RND (1) + 1):C =  INT (6 *  RND (1) + 1)
160 B(R,C) = 0:S = S + P(R,C)
170   NEXT L
180   FOR R = 1 TO 6: FOR C = 1 TO 6
190   IF B(R,C) = 0 THEN  PRINT " X ";: GOTO 210
200   PRINT " ";B(R,C);" ";
210   NEXT C: PRINT : PRINT : NEXT R
220   PRINT : PRINT "      SCORE=";S
```

23.
```
10   DIM A$(26)
20   FOR X = 1 TO 26
30   READ A$(X)
40   NEXT X
50   DATA  A,B,C,D,E,F,G,H,I,J,K,L,M,N,O,P,Q,R,S,T,U,V,W,X,Y,Z
60   FOR W = 1 TO 15
70 R =  INT (7 *  RND (1) + 1)
80   FOR L = 1 TO R
90 W$ = W$ + A$( INT (26 *  RND (1) + 1))
100  NEXT L
110  PRINT W$
120 W$ = ""
130  NEXT W
```

CHAPTER FIVE

1.
```
10   INPUT N
20   IF N < 0 THEN 40
30   PRINT "N = ";N,"SQUARE ROOTS = + OR - "; SQR (N): GOTO 10
40   PRINT N;" IS A NEGATIVE NUMBER": GOTO 10
```

3.
```
]PRINT 3^2^3          ]PRINT 5-4^2        ]PRINT 3*(5+16)
729.000003            -11                 60

]PRINT 5+3*6/2        ]PRINT 640/10/2*5   ]PRINT 5+3*4-1
14                    160                 16

]PRINT 2^3^2     ]PRINT 2^(3^2)    ]PRINT 64/4*0.5+((1+5)*2^3)*1/(2*4)
64               512.000002        14
```

5.
```
10   INPUT N
20   PRINT  SGN (N) * N
```

7.
```
10   PRINT "RADIANS","DEGREES"
20   FOR A - 0 TO 3 STEP 0.25
30   PRINT A,A * 180 / 3.1415926535
40   NEXT A
```

9.
```
10   INPUT N
15 N = N * 3.14159 / 180
20 N1 =  COS (N)
30 N2 =  SIN (N)
40 N3 =  TAN (N)
50  IF N1 > N2 AND N1 > N3 THEN  PRINT "COSINE=";N1: END
60  IF N2 > N1 AND N2 > N3 THEN  PRINT "SINE=";N2: END
70  PRINT "TANGENT=";N3
```

11.
```
10   DEF  FN Y(X) = 9 * X ^ 3 - 7 * X * X + 4 * X - 1
20   INPUT "A AND B?";A,B
30   PRINT  FN Y(B) -  FN Y(A)
```

13.
```
10   PRINT "X"; TAB( 10);"LN(X)"; TAB( 25);"EXP(X)"
15   PRINT
20   FOR X = 1 TO 15
30   PRINT X; TAB( 7); LOG (X); TAB( 22); EXP (X)
40   NEXT X
```

15.
```
]RUN
5                -4               3                4
```

17.
```
]RUN
FNF(-4) IS NEGATIVE
FNF(-2) IS NEGATIVE
FNF(0) IS NEGATIVE
FNF(2) IS ZERO
FNF(4) IS POSITIVE
FNF(6) IS POSITIVE
```

19.
```
]RUN
-3               -2               -1               0
1                2                3                4
```

21.
```
10   PRINT "NUMBER","SQUARE ROOT"
20   FOR X = 1 TO 100
30   PRINT X, SQR (X)
40   NEXT X
```

23A.
```
10   PRINT " X"; TAB( 7);"EXP(X)"; TAB( 25);"LOG(EXP(X))"
20   FOR X =  - 5 TO 10
30   PRINT X; TAB( 5); EXP (X); TAB( 22); LOG ( EXP (X))
40   NEXT X
```

23B.
```
10   PRINT " X"; TAB( 7);"LOG(X)"; TAB( 25);"EXP(LOG(X))"
20   FOR X = 1 TO 151 STEP 10
30   PRINT X; TAB( 5); LOG (X); TAB( 22); EXP ( LOG (X))
40   NEXT X
```

23C. Yes, $f(f^{-1}(x))=x$ and $f^{-1}(f(x))=x$.

23D. No; the logarithm of zero or of a negative value does not exist.

25.
```
10 P = 0.50
20 P = P *  EXP (0.08 * 10)
30  FOR X = 11 TO 50
35 P = P - .05
40 P = P *  EXP (0.08 * 1)
50  NEXT X
60  PRINT "AFTER 50 YEARS, DENNIS HAS $";P
```

27.
```
10  INPUT "X,Y?";X,Y
20 R =  SQR (X * X + Y * Y)
30  IF X = 0 THEN T = 90 *  SGN (Y): GOTO 60
40 T =  ATN (Y / X)
50 T = T * 180 / 3.1415926535
60  IF X < 0 THEN T = T + 180: GOTO 80
70  IF T < 0 THEN T = T + 360
80  PRINT "R=";R
90  PRINT "T=";T
100  GOTO 10
```

29.
```
10  INPUT "YOUR NUMBER? ";X
20 A1 =  ATN (X)
30 A2 =  ATN (X /  SQR (1 - X ^ 2))
40 A3 =  ATN ( SQR (1 - X ^ 2) / X)
50  PRINT A2,A3,A1
```

CHAPTER SIX

1.
```
10  GR : COLOR= 9
20  HLIN 19,21 AT 10
30  HLIN 19,21 AT 11
```

3.
```
10  GR : COLOR= 14
20  PLOT 15,18
30  VLIN 20,25 AT 15
```

5.
```
10  HGR : HCOLOR= 6
20  HPLOT 250,20 TO 250,110 TO 130,140 TO 250,20
```

7.
```
10  HGR : HCOLOR= 6
20  HPLOT 10,10 TO 130,110 TO 130,10
30  HPLOT  TO 70,10 TO 70,110
40  HPLOT  TO 10,110 TO 10,10
```

```
9.  10  HGR2 : HCOLOR= 5
    20 X0 = 135:Y0 = 100
    30  REM  DRAW AXES
    40  HPLOT 0,Y0 TO 279,Y0
    50  HPLOT X0,0 TO X0,191
    60  REM  GRAPH FUNCTION
    65  HCOLOR= 3
    70  FOR X1 = 0 TO 279
    80 X = X1 - X0
    90 Y = 2 ^ X
    100 Y1 = Y0 - Y
    110  IF (Y1 >  = 0) AND (Y1 <  = 191) THEN  HPLOT X1,Y1
    120  NEXT X1
```

```
11. 10  GR : COLOR= 1: HOME
    20  FOR U = 0 TO 3
    30  READ N$,A,B,C,D,E,F,G
    40 R = (A + B + C + D + E + F + G) / 7
    50  VLIN 39,39 -  INT (R) AT 10 * U
    60  VLIN 39,39 -  INT (R) AT 10 * U + 1
    70  PRINT  TAB( U * 10 + 1);N$;: NEXT U
    80  DATA  GREER,18,12,9,10,16,22,14
    90  DATA  MCPHERSON,12,21,19,16,28,20,22
    100  DATA  RADY,18,20,14,19,11,16,23
    110  DATA  WYNCOTT,23,27,18,16,21,14,24
```

```
13. 10  GR
    20  FOR N = 1 TO 5: COLOR= N
    30 X1 = 9 + 2 * N:X2 = 30 - 2 * N
    40 Y1 = 9 + 2 * N:Y2 = 30 - 2 * N
    50  HLIN X1,X2 AT Y1
    60  HLIN X1,X2 AT Y1 + 1
    70  HLIN X1,X2 AT Y2
    80  HLIN X1,X2 AT Y2 - 1
    90  VLIN Y1,Y2 AT X1
    100  VLIN Y1,Y2 AT X1 + 1
    110  VLIN Y1,Y2 AT X2
    120  VLIN Y1,Y2 AT X2 - 1
    130  NEXT N: COLOR= 0
    140  FOR S = 1 TO 10
    150 X =  INT ( RND (1) * 18) + 11
    160 Y =  INT ( RND (1) * 18) + 11
    170 T = T +  SCRN( X,Y)
    180  PLOT X,Y: NEXT S
    190  PRINT "TOTAL SCORE =";T
```

15A.
```
10  HGR2 : HCOLOR= 5
20 XO = 135:YO = 100
30  REM  DRAW AXES
40  HPLOT O,YO TO 279,YO
50  HPLOT XO,0 TO XO,191
60  REM  SCALE GRAPH OF Y=SGN(X)
64  REM  BY MULTIPYING Y BY 5
66  HCOLOR= 3
70  FOR X1 = 0 TO 279
80 X = X1 - XO
90 Y =  SGN (X) * 5
100 Y1 = YO - Y
110  IF (Y1 >  = 0) AND (Y1 <  = 191) THEN  HPLOT X1,Y1
120  NEXT X1
```

15B.
```
10  HGR2 : HCOLOR= 5
20 XO = 135:YO = 100
30  REM  DRAW AXES
40  HPLOT O,YO TO 279,YO
50  HPLOT XO,0 TO XO,191
60  REM  SCALE GRAPH OF Y=ATN(X) BY MULTIPLYING Y BY 50
65  HCOLOR= 3
70  FOR X1 = 0 TO 279
80 X = X1 - XO
90 Y =  ATN (X) * 50
100 Y1 = YO - Y
110  IF (Y1 >  = 0) AND (Y1 <  = 191) THEN  HPLOT X1,Y1
120  NEXT X1
```

15C.
```
10  HGR2 : HCOLOR= 5
20 XO = 135:YO = 100
30  REM  DRAW AXES
40  HPLOT O,YO TO 279,YO
50  HPLOT XO,0 TO XO,191
60  REM  PLOT GRAPH OF Y=INT(X)
62  REM  NOTICE THE X STEP OF 0.5
65  HCOLOR= 3
70  FOR X1 = 0 TO 279 STEP 0.5
80 X = X1 - XO
90 Y =  INT (X)
100 Y1 = YO - Y
110  IF (Y1 >  = 0) AND (Y1 <  = 191) THEN  HPLOT X1,Y1
120  NEXT X1
```

17A.
```
10   REM  TOWERS OF HANOI
20   REM  GRAPHICS CHAPTER
30   REM
40   REM   PLOT THE BASE AND PEGS IN GREEN
50   REM
60   HOME : GR : COLOR= 12
70   FOR X = 33 TO 35: HLIN 2,36 AT X: NEXT X
80   VLIN 20,33 AT 8
90   VLIN 20,33 AT 19: VLIN 20,33 AT 30
100  REM
110  REM  PLOT THE 5 DISCS
120  REM
130  COLOR= 1: FOR X = 1 TO 5
140  HLIN 8 - X,8 + X AT 2 * X + 22
150  NEXT X
```

17B.
```
10   REM  TOWERS OF HANOI PROBLEM
20   REM       GRAPHICS CHAPTER
30   REM
40   REM   PLOT THE BASE AND PEGS IN GREEN
50   REM
60   HOME : GR : COLOR= 12: DIM A(3,5)
70   FOR X = 33 TO 35: HLIN 2,36 AT X: NEXT X
80   VLIN 20,33 AT 8
90   VLIN 20,33 AT 19: VLIN 20,33 AT 30
100  REM
110  REM  INITIALIZE 3 ARRAYS FOR EACH PEG
120  REM
130  COLOR= 1: FOR X = 1 TO 5
140  HLIN 8 - X,8 + X AT 2 * X + 22
150 A(1,X) = X:A(2,X) = 0:A(3,X) = 0
160  NEXT X
170  REM
180  REM   MOVEMENT OF DISKS
190  REM
200  INPUT "FROM TOWER, TO TOWER? ";T1,T2
210 DISK = 0: FOR X = 1 TO 5
220  IF DISK > 0 OR A(T1,X) = 0 THEN 260
230 DISK = A(T1,X):XCTR = 8 + (T1 - 1) * 11:A(T1,X) = 0
240  COLOR= 0: HLIN XCTR - DISK,XCTR + DISK AT 2 * X + 22
250  COLOR= 12: PLOT XCTR,2 * X + 22: COLOR= 1
260  NEXT X
270  IF DISK = 0 THEN  PRINT "NO DISK THERE!": GOTO 200
280 EMPTY = 0: FOR X = 5 TO 1 STEP  - 1
290  IF EMPTY = 0 AND A(T2,X) = 0 THEN EMPTY = X
300  NEXT X: IF EMPTY = 5 THEN 330
310  IF A(T2,EMPTY + 1) >  = DISK THEN 330
320  PRINT "YOU CAN'T DO THAT!":T2 = T1: GOTO 280
330  REM  PLOT THE DISK AT A(T2,EMPTY)
340 X = 8 + (T2 - 1) * 11:Y = 2 * EMPTY + 22
350  COLOR= 1: HLIN X - DISK,X + DISK AT Y
360 A(T2,EMPTY) = DISK
370  PRINT : IF T2 = 1 OR EMPTY <  > 1 THEN 200
380  PRINT "GOOD SHOW OL' CHAP!"
```

Note: For the sake of clarity, some of the variable names used in this program have more than one letter.

CHAPTER SEVEN

1.
```
10  GOSUB 400
20  FOR J = 1 TO 40
30  PRINT "*";
40  NEXT J
50  GOSUB 400
60  FOR J = 1 TO 3
70  PRINT "!",
80  NEXT J
90  GOSUB 400
100  FOR J = 1 TO 20
110  PRINT "AB";
120  NEXT J
130  END
400  PRINT
410 I = I + 1
420  PRINT "PART ";I
430  RETURN
```

3.
```
10 A$ = "YOU HAVE WON A "
20 R =  INT (1 + 4 *  RND (1))
30  ON R GOTO 40,60,80,100
40  PRINT A$;"BALL"
50  END
60  PRINT A$;"BALLOON"
70  END
80  PRINT A$;"TOY CAR"
90  END
100  PRINT A$;"CANDY BAR"
```

5.
```
10 A$ = "1234567890"
20  FOR L = 1 TO 4
30  PRINT A$;
40  NEXT L
```

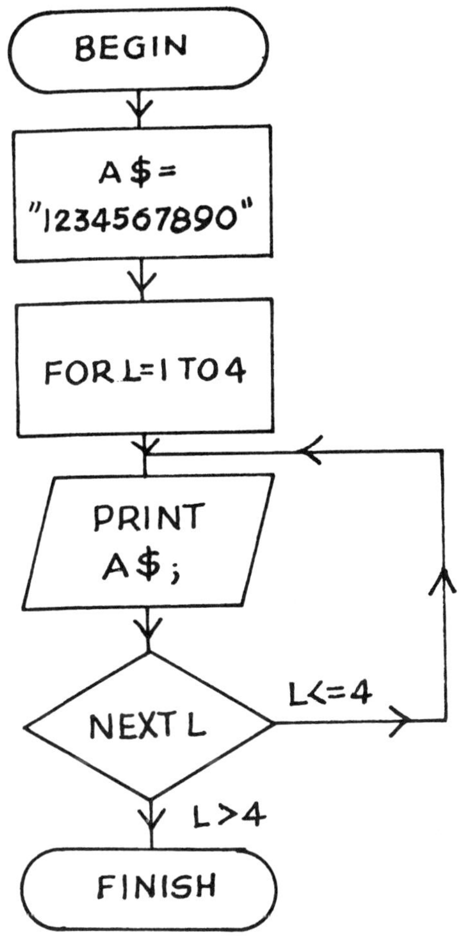

7.
```
10  INPUT X
20  IF  ABS (X) < 1 THEN  GOTO 10
30 N =  INT (X)
40 I = I + 1
50  IF I <  = N THEN  PRINT "REPEAT": GOTO 40
60  PRINT "FINISHED"
```

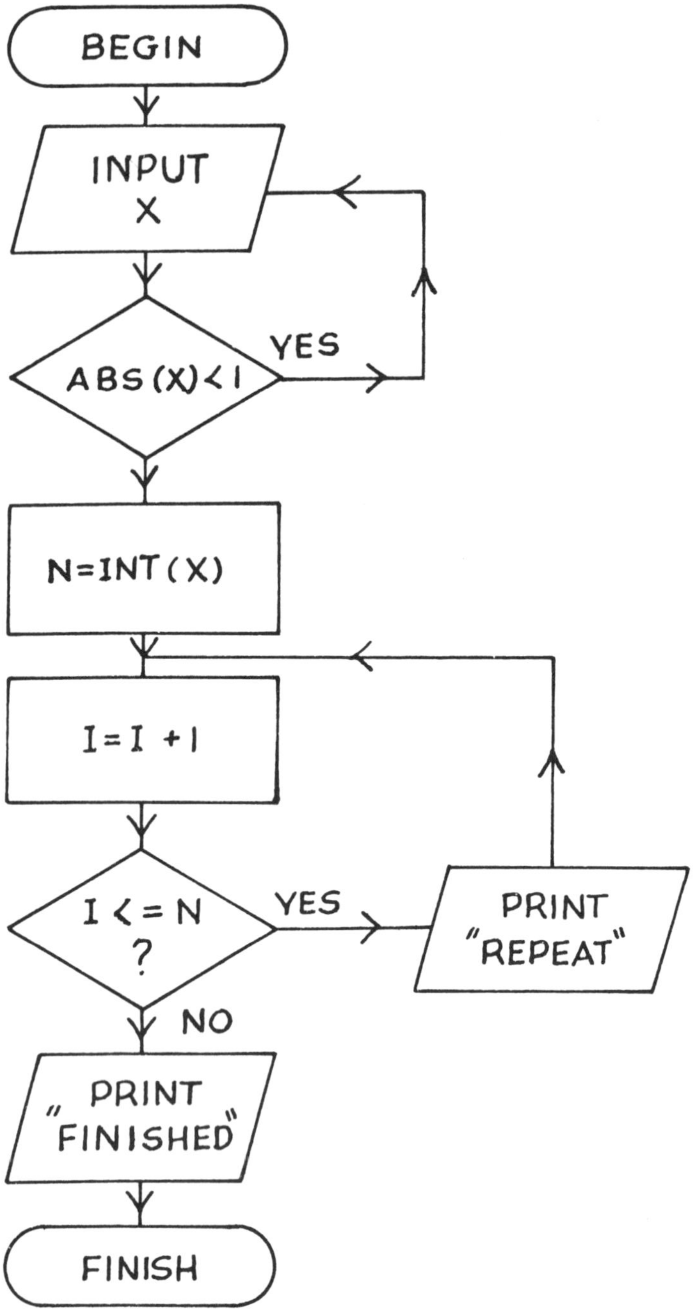

9.

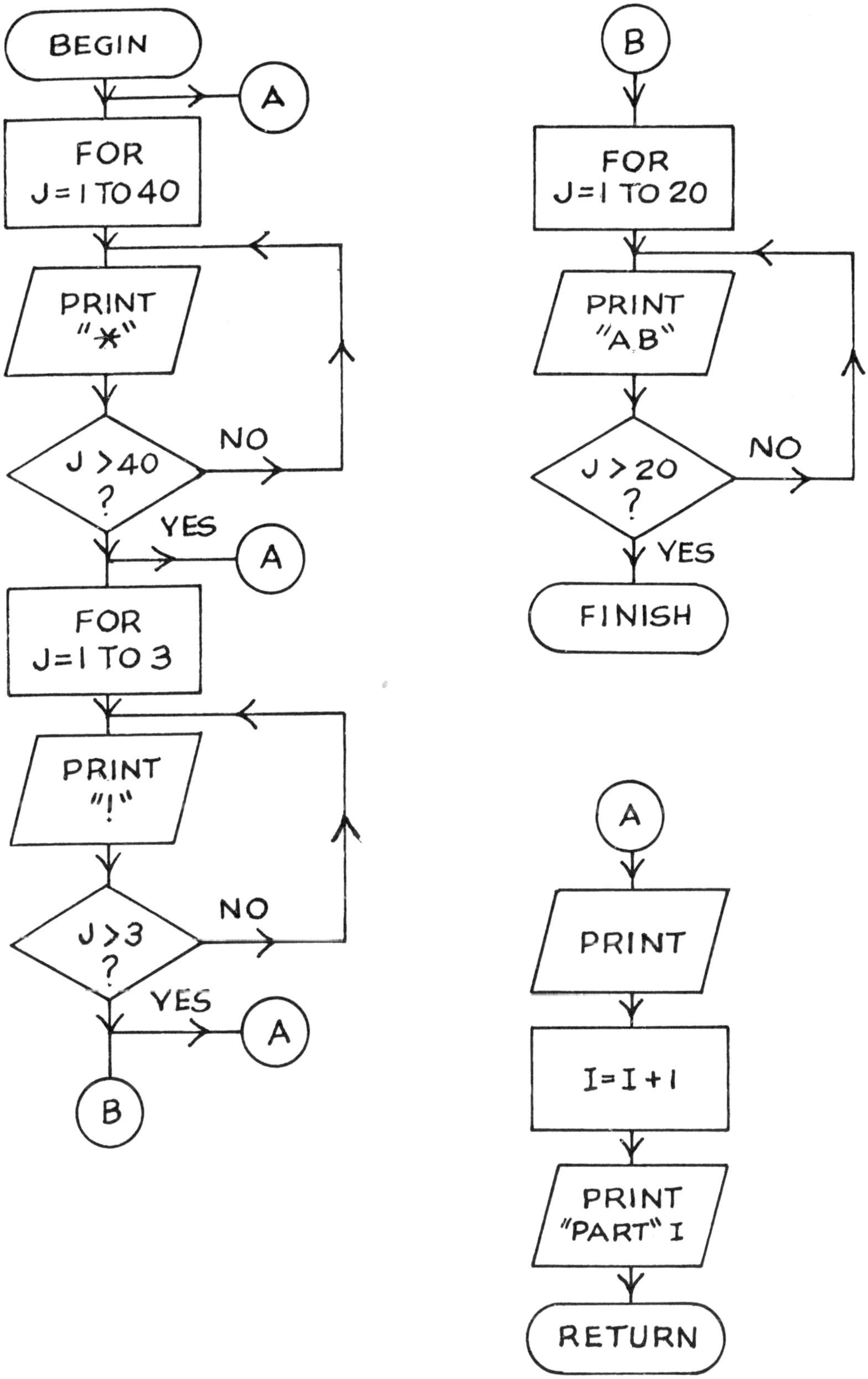

BEGIN
A
FOR
J=1 TO 40
PRINT
"*"
J >40
?
NO
YES
A
FOR
J=1 TO 3
PRINT
"!"
J >3
?
NO
YES
A
B
B
FOR
J=1 TO 20
PRINT
"AB"
J >20
?
NO
YES
FINISH
A
PRINT
I=I+1
PRINT
"PART" I
RETURN

11A. The lines are executed in the following order:

10,20,30,70,40,10,20,30,50,40,10,20,30,60,40,10,20,90

11B.
```
]80 DATA 3,0,4,-5,-1,-8,1,5,999

]RUN
N = 3              Z = 1              P = 4
```

13A. The lines are executed in the following order:

10,20,30,60,70,80,40,50,10,20,30,60,70,80,40,50,
10,20,30,60,80,40,50,10,20,95

13B.
```
]90 DATA 1,8,-2,5,-3,-6,2,4,-7,0

]RUN
T = 2              P = 20
```

15.
```
10 X =  INT ( - 5 + 11 *  RND (1)):Y =  INT ( - 5 + 11 *  RND (1))
20  FOR I = 1 TO 3
30  INPUT "TWO INTEGERS BETWEEN -5 AND 5, INCLUSIVE? ";X1,Y1
40  GOSUB 140
50  IF D = 0 THEN  END
60  NEXT I
70 X1 = X: PRINT "X = ";X
80  FOR J = 1 TO 2
90  INPUT "Y1? ";Y1
100  GOSUB 140
110  IF D = 0 THEN  END
120  NEXT J
130  PRINT "YOU FAILED. Y = ";Y
135  END
140 D =  SQR ((X - X1) ^ 2 + (Y - Y1) ^ 2)
150  PRINT D
160  IF D = 0 THEN  PRINT "CORRECT"
170  RETURN
```

17.
```
10  INPUT "WITHDRAWL (1), DEPOSIT (2), OR CALULATE INTEREST(3)
? ";D
20  ON D GOSUB 120,150,180
30  PRINT "YOUR BALANCE NOW STANDS AT ";B;" DOLLARS."
40  GOTO 10
120  INPUT "HOW MUCH WOULD YOU LIKE TO WITHDRAW? ";A
130  IF A >  = 0 AND B - A > 0 THEN B = B - A: RETURN
140  GOTO 120
150  INPUT "HOW MUCH WOULD YOU LIKE TO DEPOSIT? ";A
160  IF A >  = 0 THEN B = B + A: RETURN
170  GOTO 150
180  INPUT "HOW MANY MONTHS SINCE LAST CALCULATION? ";M
190 Q = M / 4
200  IF Q < 1 THEN  PRINT "TOO SOON": RETURN
210  FOR C = 1 TO Q
220 B = B + .0575 * B
230  NEXT C
240  RETURN
```

19.
```
10  READ A,B,C
20 S = (A + B + C) / 2
30 A =  SQR (S * (S - A) * (S - B) * (S - C))
40  PRINT "AREA = ";A
50  GOTO 10
100  DATA  5,8,12
110  DATA  8,13,20
120  DATA  13,21,33
```

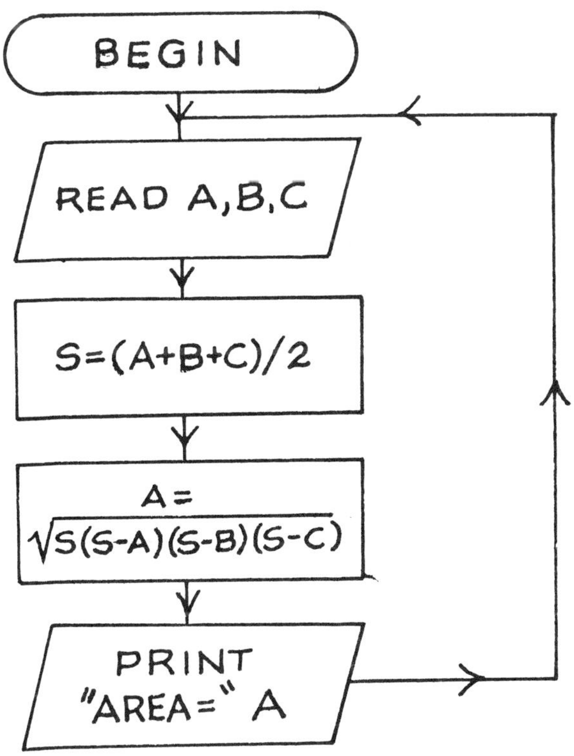

21.
```
10   PRINT "AN ";: GOSUB 100
20   PRINT " A DAY KEEPS THE DOCTOR AWAY."
30   PRINT "IS THERE A BUG IN YOUR ";: GOSUB 100
40   PRINT "?"
50   PRINT "HOW DO YOU LIKE THEM ";
60   GOSUB 100
70   PRINT "S?!"
80   PRINT "DON'T LET YOUR ";: GOSUB 100
90   PRINT " ROT!"
95   END
100  FLASH : PRINT "APPLE";: NORMAL
110  RETURN
```

CHAPTER EIGHT

1A.
```
10   DIM R(50):DOS$ =  CHR$ (4)
20   FOR X = 1 TO 50
30 R(X) =  INT (20 *  RND (1) + 1)
40   NEXT X
50   PRINT DOS$;"OPEN RANUM"
60   PRINT DOS$;"WRITE RANUM"
70   FOR I = 1 TO 50
80   PRINT R(I)
90   NEXT I
100  PRINT DOS$;"CLOSE RANUM"
```

1B.
```
10 DOS$ =  CHR$ (4)
20   PRINT DOS$;"OPEN RANUM"
30   PRINT DOS$;"READ RANUM"
40   FOR I = 1 TO 50
50   INPUT R
60 S = S + R
70   NEXT I
80   PRINT DOS$;"CLOSE RANUM"
90   PRINT S
```

3A.
```
10 DOS$ =  CHR$ (4)
20   FOR X = 1 TO 10
30   INPUT "NAME? ";N$(X)
40   NEXT X
50   PRINT DOS$;"OPEN TNM"
60   PRINT DOS$;"WRITE TNM"
70   FOR I = 1 TO 10
80   PRINT N$(I)
90   NEXT I
100  PRINT DOS$;"CLOSE TNM"
```

3B.
```
10 DOS$ =  CHR$ (4):X =  - 1
20  PRINT DOS$;"OPEN TNM"
30  PRINT DOS$;"READ TNM"
40  FOR P = 1 TO 10
50  INPUT N$
60  IF N$ > "C" AND N$ < "I" THEN  PRINT N$:X = X + 2
70  NEXT P
80  PRINT DOS$;"CLOSE TNM"
90  IF X < 0 THEN  PRINT "NONE FOUND"
```

5A.
```
10 DOS$ =  CHR$ (4)
20  FOR X = 1 TO 10
30  INPUT "TITLE? ";T$(X)
40  NEXT X
50  PRINT DOS$;"OPEN BOOKS,L60"
60  FOR I = 1 TO 10
70  PRINT DOS$;"WRITE BOOKS,R";I
80  PRINT T$(I)
90  NEXT I
100  PRINT DOS$;"CLOSE BOOKS"
```

5B.
```
10 DOS$ =  CHR$ (4)
20  PRINT DOS$;"OPEN BOOKS,L60"
30  PRINT DOS$;"OPEN N-Z TITLES"
40  FOR B = 1 TO 10
50  PRINT DOS$;"READ BOOKS,R";B
60  INPUT T$
70  IF T$ < "N" THEN 100
90  PRINT DOS$;"WRITE N-Z TITLES"
95  PRINT T$
100  NEXT B
110  PRINT DOS$;"CLOSE BOOKS"
120  PRINT DOS$;"CLOSE N-Z TITLES"
```

7A.
```
10 DOS$ =  CHR$ (4): DIM N$(25): DIM B(25)
20  FOR A = 1 TO 25
30  PRINT "ACCOUNT #";A
40  INPUT "NAME: ";N$(A)
50  INPUT "BALANCE: ";B(A)
60  NEXT A
70  PRINT DOS$;"OPEN ACCOUNTS,L25"
80  FOR C = 1 TO 25
90  PRINT DOS$;"WRITE ACCOUNTS,R";C
100  PRINT N$(C): PRINT B(C)
110  NEXT C
120  PRINT DOS$;"CLOSE ACCOUNTS"
```

7B.
```
10 DOS$ =  CHR$ (4)
20  PRINT DOS$;"OPEN ACCOUNTS,L25"
30  INPUT "ACCOUNT NUMBER? ";A
40  PRINT DOS$;"READ ACCOUNTS,R";A
50  INPUT N$: INPUT B
60  PRINT DOS$
70  PRINT N$;"'S CURRENT BALANCE IS ";B
80  INPUT "DEPOSIT (D) OR WITHDRAWEL (W)? ";T$
90  INPUT "AMOUNT? ";T
100  IF T$ = "W" THEN T =  - T
110 B = B + T
120  PRINT "NEW BALANCE IS ";B
130  PRINT DOS$;"WRITE ACCOUNTS,R";A
140  PRINT N$: PRINT B
150  PRINT DOS$;"CLOSE ACCOUNTS"
160  PRINT : PRINT "TRANSACTION COMPLETE"
```

7C.
```
10 DOS$ =  CHR$ (4)
20  PRINT DOS$;"OPEN ACCOUNTS,L25"
30  FOR A = 1 TO 25
40  PRINT DOS$;"READ ACCOUNTS,R";A
50  INPUT N$: INPUT B
60  IF B < 0 THEN 90
70  IF B >  = 500 THEN 150
80  NEXT A: PRINT DOS$;"CLOSE ACCOUNTS": END
90  PRINT : PRINT "DEAR ";N$
100  PRINT "      YOUR ACCOUNT IS OVER DRAWN"
110  PRINT "BY "; - B;" DOLLARS.  PLEASE MAKE A"
120  PRINT "DEPOSIT FOR THAT AMOUNT IMMEDIATELY."
130  PRINT : PRINT "                         THE BANK"
140  PRINT : GOTO 80
150  PRINT : PRINT "DEAR ";N$
160  PRINT "CONGRATULATIONS!  YOUR BALANCE"
170  PRINT "IS ";B;" DOLLARS.  YOU WILL BE"
180  PRINT "RECEIVING A TOASTER IN THE MAIL."
190  PRINT : PRINT "                         THE BANK"
200  GOTO 80
```

9A.
```
10 DOS$ =  CHR$ (4): DIM N$(30),F$(30),A(30)
20  PRINT DOS$;"OPEN FRAT,L40"
30  FOR X = 1 TO 30
40  INPUT "NAME? ";N$(X)
50  INPUT "FRATERNITY? ";F$(X)
60  INPUT "AGE? ";A(X)
70  NEXT X
80  FOR Q = 1 TO 30
90  PRINT DOS$;"WRITE FRAT,R";Q
100  PRINT N$(Q): PRINT F$(Q): PRINT A(Q)
110  NEXT Q
120  PRINT DOS$;"CLOSE FRAT"
```

9B.
```
10 DOS$ =  CHR$ (4)
20  PRINT DOS$;"OPEN FRAT,L40"
30  PRINT DOS$;"OPEN SIGMA"
40  FOR X = 1 TO 30
50  PRINT DOS$;"READ FRAT,R";X
60  INPUT N$: INPUT F$: INPUT A
70  IF F$ = "SIGMA CHI" THEN 120
80  NEXT X
90  PRINT DOS$;"CLOSE FRAT"
100  PRINT DOS$;"CLOSE SIGMA"
110  END
120  PRINT DOS$;"WRITE SIGMA"
130  PRINT N$: PRINT A
140  GOTO 80
```

9C.
```
10 DOS$ =  CHR$ (4): DIM P(30): DIM S$(5,5)
20  PRINT DOS$;"OPEN FRAT,L40"
30  FOR X = 1 TO 5: FOR Y = 1 TO 5
40 R =  INT (30 *  RND (1) + 1)
50  IF P(R) = 1 THEN 40
60 P(R) = 1: PRINT DOS$;"READ FRAT,R";R
70  INPUT N$:S$(X,Y) = N$
80  NEXT Y: NEXT X
90  PRINT DOS$;"CLOSE FRAT"
100  FOR X = 1 TO 5: FOR Y = 1 TO 5
110  PRINT  TAB( (Y - 1) * 7 + 1);S$(X,Y);
120  NEXT Y: PRINT : NEXT X
```

11A.
```
10 DOS$ =  CHR$ (4)
20  PRINT DOS$;"OPEN PAY"
30  PRINT DOS$;"WRITE PAY"
40  FOR X = 1 TO 10
50  READ N$,R,D,M,L
60  PRINT N$: PRINT R: PRINT D
70  PRINT M: PRINT L: NEXT X
80  PRINT DOS$;"CLOSE PAY"
90  DATA  "ISLAND GILLIGAN",-4.50,0,2,1
100  DATA  "WILSON MISTER",4.95,2,5,3
110  DATA "MENACE DENNIS",1,0,2,1
120  DATA  "BEAVER LEAVEITTO",2.25,0,1,1
130  DATA  "FREJTAG ALEX",-0.01,5,0,6
140  DATA  "HOGAN COLONEL",40,2,3,3
150  DATA  "SHULTZ SERGEANT",30,1,1,2
160  DATA  "BANNER JOHN",20,1,0,2
170  DATA  "KIRK JIM",78.50,1,1,1
180  DATA  "BUNNY BUGS",12.45,2,5,3
190  DATA  "SERLING ROD",55.90,2,2,1
200  DATA  "TARZAN ME",9,25,3,0,0
```

11B.
```
10 DOS$ =  CHR$ (4)
20  DEF  FN R(X) =  INT (100 * X + .5) / 100
30  PRINT DOS$;"OPEN PAY"
40  PRINT DOS$;"READ PAY"
50  FOR X = 1 TO 10
60  INPUT N$: INPUT R: INPUT D
70  INPUT M: INPUT L: READ H
80 G = H * R
90 T = (25 - 2 * D) * G / 100
100  IF T < 0 THEN T = 0
110 P = G - T - M - L
120  PRINT N$;" HRS:";H;" GP:"; FN R(G);" TX:"; FN R(T);
130  PRINT " MI:"; FN R(M);" LI:"; FN R(L);" NET:"; FN R(P)
140  NEXT X
150  DATA  40,37.1,51,48,39.2,18.6,59.8,45.3,68.3,41
160  PRINT DOS$;"CLOSE PAY"
```

CHAPTER NINE

1.
```
10  PRINT "X","10^X","2^X"
20  FOR X = 5 TO  - 5 STEP  - 1
30  PRINT X,10 ^ X,2 ^ X
40  NEXT X
```

3.
```
10  DATA  65,83,67,73,73,32,68,73,68,32
15  DATA  84,72,73,83,33
20  FOR I = 1 TO 15
30  READ X: PRINT  CHR$ (X);
40  NEXT I
```

5.
```
10 A$ = "THREE!@#$%STRING!@#$%FUNCTIONS"
20 L$ =  LEFT$ (A$,5)
30 M$ =  MID$ (A$,11,6)
40 R$ =  RIGHT$ (A$,9)
50  PRINT L$;" ";M$;" ";R$
```

7.
```
10  INPUT "YOUR STRING? ";A$
20  FOR L =  LEN (A$) TO 1 STEP  - 1
30 A =  ASC ( RIGHT$ (A$,L))
40  PRINT A;"  ";
50  NEXT L
```

9.
```
10  DATA  QUEEN, LENGTH, REMEMBER
20  READ A$
30 K =  LEN (A$)
40  FOR I = 1 TO K
50 B$ =  MID$ (A$,I,1)
60  IF B$ = "E" THEN 80
70  PRINT B$;
80  NEXT I
90  PRINT
100  GOTO 20
```

11.

BINARY	DECIMAL
1011	11
10100	20
1111	15
1110	14
1010011	83
110011	51
1011100	92
1101111	111
11000000	192
10000111	135

13.
```
10  FOR C =  ASC ("A") TO  ASC ("L")
20 A$ = A$ +  CHR$ (C)
30  NEXT C
40  FOR X = 1 TO 12
50  PRINT  LEFT$ (A$,X)
60  NEXT X
```

15.
```
]RUN
87
72
55
54
```

17.
```
10  FOR X = 1 TO 15
20 C =  RND (1) * 26 + 65
30  PRINT  CHR$ (C);
40  NEXT X
```

19.
```
10  FOR X = 1 TO 100
20 A$ = A$ +  CHR$ ( INT ( RND (1) * 95) + 32)
30  NEXT X
40  FOR I = 1 TO 100:C =  ASC ( MID$ (A$,I,1))
50  IF (C > 64 AND C < 91) OR (C > 96 AND C < 123) THEN L = L +
1: GOTO 80
60  IF C > 47 AND C < 58 THEN N = N + 1: GOTO 80
70 M = M + 1
80  NEXT I
90  PRINT "THERE ARE ";L;" LETTERS, ";N;" NUMBERS, AND ";M;" MIS
CELLANEOUS CHARACTERS."
```

21A.
```
10  INPUT "MESSAGE TO ENCODE? ";M$
20  FOR I = 1 TO  LEN (M$):C =  ASC ( MID$ (M$,I,1))
30  IF C < 65 OR C > 90 THEN 60
40 C = C + 2
50  IF C > 90 THEN C = C - 26
60 A$ = A$ +  CHR$ (C)
70  NEXT I
80  PRINT "ENCODED MESSAGE: ";A$
```

21B.
```
10  INPUT "MESSAGE TO DECODE? ";M$
20  FOR I = 1 TO  LEN (M$):C =  ASC ( MID$ (M$,I,1))
30  IF C < 65 OR C > 90 THEN 60
40 C = C - 2
50  IF C < 65 THEN C = C + 26
60 A$ = A$ +  CHR$ (C)
70  NEXT I
80  PRINT "MESSAGE: ";A$
```

23.
```
10  DIM S$(30),N(9)
15 C = C + 1
20  PRINT "SENTENCE? ";
25  GET A$: PRINT A$;: IF  ASC (A$) = 13 THEN 30
27 S$(C) = S$(C) + A$
28  GOTO 25
30  IF  LEN (S$(C)) = 0 THEN 50
40 S$(C) =  CHR$ (32) + S$(C) +  CHR$ (32)
45  GOTO 15
50  FOR L = 1 TO C - 1
60  RESTORE
65  FOR W = 1 TO 9
70  READ T$
80  GOSUB 125
90 N(W) = N(W) + R
100  NEXT W
110  NEXT L
115  GOTO 160
120  DATA    " A "," AN "," THE "," LY ",".","!","?",";",","
125 R = 0
130  FOR P = 1 TO  LEN (S$(L))
140  IF  MID$ (S$(L),P, LEN (T$)) = T$ THEN R = R + 1
150  NEXT P
155  RETURN
160  PRINT "ARTICLES: ";N(1) + N(2) + N(3)
170  PRINT "ADVERBS: ";N(4)
180  PRINT "PUNCTUATION MARKS: ";N(5) + N(6) + N(7) + N(8) + N(9)
```

25.
```
10 C = C + 1
20  PRINT "WHAT IS YOUR ";C;
30  INPUT " WORD? ";W$(C)
40  IF  LEN (W$(C)) > 0 THEN 10
50  FOR L = 1 TO C - 1
60  PRINT  CHR$ ( ASC (W$(L)));
70  NEXT L
80  PRINT
90 C = 0: GOTO 10
```

27.
```
10  INPUT "WHAT IS YOUR BINARY NUMBER? ";N$
20 D = 0
30  FOR I = 1 TO  LEN (N$)
40  IF  ASC ( MID$ (N$,I,1)) = 49 THEN D = D + 2 ^ ( LEN (N$) -
I)
50  NEXT I
60  PRINT "IT'S DECIMAL EQUIVALENT IS ";D
70  GOTO 10
```

INDEX